Advance praise for *Viking for Life*

"He was not big enough, strong enough, or fast enough; all he was, was good enough. He proved everyone wrong. While playing 14 years in the National Football League, he missed few games. We always knew he had the quality of durability, and you do not achieve greatness without durability. Scott worked his way into our starting lineup and played at the highest level. He set the highest of standards for our football team."

—Bud Grant, Vikings head coach from 1967 to 1983 and in 1985

"Scott's passion, work ethic, and intelligence made him a great player on the field, and these attributes carried over to what he did in the front office for the Minnesota Vikings. Forty-two years of outstanding work and excellence tell his story. His leadership and contributions will always be remembered."

—Rick Spielman, Vikings general manager

"Scott was a tackling machine. He would do absolutely everything possible to get to the ball carrier. On the field he was a great leader. He always got us in the right position, and was the smartest ballplayer I have ever played with or against. Besides being an outstanding player for the Vikings, he is an even better person."

—Keith Millard, Vikings defensive tackle from 1985 to 1991

"When thinking about Scott, one word comes to mind: stud. We lined up next to each other for 11 of the 14 years that he played for the Vikings. His friendship and leadership impacted me more than anything and will dwell in my heart forever. No one in my life has had a greater impact on me and my family. He will always be my brother."

—Mark Mullancy, Vikings defensive end from 1975 to 1986

"I played with Joe Schmidt in Detroit, who was one of the best ever. Scott reminds me a lot of Joe. He was the signal caller on defense for the Vikings forever. He did a tremendous job and was respected by everyone. When we drafted him, we had no idea he would become the great leader and player that he was. Besides holding those football standards, he is one of the finest people you would ever want to meet."

—Jerry Reichow, Vikings wide receiver from 1961 to 1964 and longtime Vikings scout

"The one thing I will always remember about Scott is that he was bloody all the time. We were roommates for six years and are still great friends to this day. As a player he was mean and was going to hit you going full speed whenever you were on the football field. Scott was extremely smart, an excellent leader on our football team, and liked by everyone. You could never find a nicer guy."

—Tommy Kramer, Vikings quarterback from 1977 to 1989

VIKING FOR LIFE

A FOUR-DECADE FOOTBALL LOVE AFFAIR

SCOTT STUDWELL
WITH JIM BRUTON

TRIUMPH
BOOKS

I dedicate this book to my parents, Jim and Barbara Studwell, and my wife, Jenny, for their unconditional love, support, and help.

Library of Congress Cataloging-in-Publication Data available upon request.

This book is available in quantity at special discounts for your group or organization. For further information, contact:

Triumph Books LLC
814 North Franklin Street
Chicago, Illinois 60610
(312) 337-0747
www.triumphbooks.com

Printed in U.S.A.
ISBN: 978-1-62937-890-9
Design by Patricia Frey

All photos courtesy of the author unless otherwise noted

Contents

Foreword

How often do we meet a truly authentic person? Scott Studwell is one of those authentic people in my life. It has been more than 70 years since, as a high school freshman, I first donned my football cleats, shoulder pads, and helmet and became part of the team, beginning my life in football. To me, the game is a wonderful team and spectator sport. I have had the joy of participating in the excitement of some dramatic and special team victories, as well as some agonizing losses along the way.

A multitude of emotions is such a big part of the game, but I still find, in the quiet times, that it is the people I have worked with throughout my lifetime who have added so much more to the memory bank than any football-related emotion. And one of the most impressive athletic personalities I have ever crossed paths with is Scott Studwell. My favorite trait in any athlete is the inner drive to be able to will himself or herself to greatness. Scott Studwell is one of those rare individuals.

I was not part of the Vikings organization in 1977 when Scott arrived on the scene. Though I have been told that he brought with him on day one the same leadership, intelligence, commitment, and charismatic personality that has made him such a vital part of the Vikings family and community. He had great focus on everything he did in football, but he was also able to balance that with his upbeat and creative sense of humor, sometimes at his own expense.

Following his retirement as an active player, Scott continued to work with the Vikings organization. He immediately became a voice of wisdom and influence in our personnel meetings. He always had the courage to say what needed to be said and when he spoke, everyone listened.

When word came that Scott was to be enshrined into our Vikings Legends Ring of Honor, my thought was, *No one deserves it more.* There is enormous respect for Scott and all that he has contributed to our team throughout the years. He, in turn, has had great mutual respect and sincere care for his team and teammates.

Scott Studwell will always be one of my favorite players. I admire his commitment to his team and himself in reaching for greatness. And I admire the way in which he has carried his laurels of success. His authenticity, coupled with his commitment to the game, make me honored to have known and worked with him. I am proud to call him my friend. I applaud author Jim Bruton for selecting Scott for this, his next biography.

—Paul Wiggin,
consultant to pro personnel, Minnesota Vikings

CHAPTER ONE

A Great Childhood

I grew up in Evansville, Indiana. I was born in August 1954, and to this day my mom keeps telling me that it was one of the hottest days ever. I guess the temperature hit more than 100 degrees—a real scorcher. Evansville remained my home until I came to Minnesota, but there still is a touch of belonging there.

My mom and dad were high school sweethearts in Glen Ridge, New Jersey. Dad played football in high school and college, and went into the insurance business. They lived out East early in their marriage and eventually moved to Evansville, where they raised me and my three siblings. They're still there today. My mom and dad are quite the couple. They've been married more than 70 years. My dad is 92 and my mom is 90, and they are still very independent. About five years ago they took out a 30-year mortgage on their new home. For a couple of their age, that is quite an undertaking! They were unbelievably supportive to me and to my brother and sisters; they were always there for us and still are to this day.

My brother, sisters, and I were all athletes growing up. My brother, Bill, played basketball and football at the University of Evansville. My older sister, Andy, was a swimmer, and my younger sister, Sally, ran track. Bill and Sally still live in Evansville and my sister Andy lives in the Twin Cities.

My dad's dad was a military guy. We always called him Colonel. His wife was a stay-at-home mom. My mom's dad worked on Wall Street, and her mom, my grandma—"Miss Mom," we used to call her—was the sweetest and most phenomenal lady ever.

I had an incredible childhood. Growing up in the 1950s and early 1960s, I lived in a pretty laid-back neighborhood. I had a lot of fun. What I remember most about those days was going to school and playing ball with the other kids. I loved being a kid. Everything about it was the best. My dad went to work every day and my mom stayed at home and always had dinner ready for us every night. Still, Mom and Dad always found time for us kids. They were great parents.

On Sunday night we would always sit down with family and watch *Bonanza*, *Ed Sullivan*, and *Mission: Impossible*. We weren't dependent on television like many kids are today; we were always outside running around. We were a middle-class family and had a lot of friends and great neighbors. It was a very close-knit neighborhood, and there was a family kitty-corner from us named McCool. They had 10 kids and it was a free-for-all, day after day. We could always find something to do.

We didn't have organized youth football in Evansville, so the first team I joined was in the eighth grade. Cub football, as it was called, was a pilot program for Harrison High School. I followed the football team at the University of Indiana, but never closely. We were so busy doing things outside that I barely remember Saturday afternoons and college football, though I do recall watching a little football on our black-and-white television.

I was kind of a late bloomer. When I got to high school I was five foot two and 110 pounds. I wanted to play quarterback and linebacker but was a little too small for either position. My brother was just the opposite. He was only 18 months older and was more than six feet tall and weighed about 180 pounds. I was the runt.

I tried to wrestle as a freshman, got cut from the basketball team, and was actually a better baseball player than anything else. I started to grow as a sophomore and got into weight lifting. (This was a time when any kind of weight training was very limited.) I began putting on weight in the right places—as muscle mass. I would lift weights in the garage, the YMCA, or wherever else I could find them.

I gained more than 100 pounds in just a few years in high school. I also grew a foot. At least I was starting to look more like a football player. Timing-wise it was great for me. It improved my strength and my confidence, and I began to fall in love with football.

I followed in my brother's footsteps. He was a big wide receiver in high school and was pretty good. He ended up getting a scholarship to the University of Evansville. We were only one year apart and both were very competitive. I loved going at it with him.

Harrison had about 2,000 students and was one of many high schools in the area. I played on the freshman team, then really didn't play much as a sophomore. But as a junior in high school, I was playing on the varsity full-time. I played running back and linebacker. As running back I was really more of a blocking back, so I didn't carry the ball very much. Linebacker was great because I loved hitting the other players. I was also a part-time field goal kicker—but I was 0–1 in that department, so I clearly wasn't winning any games with my leg. One of my clearest memories was the semi-long field goal I missed.

To this day, I still believe I made it. The record shows I missed it, but I know deep down in my heart that the ball went 30 yards and then through the uprights, not under them.

Our high school football coach was Don Watson. He was a real character. He was a very funny, short guy with a crew cut. He could get on you when it was time, and he could love you up when the time was right too. He passed away some years ago. The assistant coaches were Don LaDue, Jim Grovanneti, and Mitch Marsh. They were a lot of fun, and they were great leaders and mentors.

Our team was average but very competitive. We never won a city title or anything like that, though in my senior season we won eight games and lost only two. We had a crosstown rival, Reitz High School, who was a powerhouse in the conference. I know we always lost to them.

I have always had great love for the game of football. I believe that I had good natural instincts for the game, things that no one is able to really teach in a player. Either you have it or you don't. I don't know why or how, but I know I had it. Perhaps I inherited it at some point from my dad or my mom.

I gained great experience playing high school football. I learned a lot about teamwork and camaraderie. For me the game came easy. Those kinds of things will happen when you love the game, are extremely competitive, have all the natural instincts, and want to win. I loved the game and I worked hard at it. I've always believed that you get out of something what you put into it. The game of football became one of the biggest loves in my life.

I made somewhat of a name for myself as a junior and started getting letters from colleges, including some of the Big Ten schools.

They were all interested in me as a linebacker. I visited Purdue, Illinois, Indiana, and Michigan, and some other midwestern schools, in addition to Louisville. I wanted to stay close to home. My parents had always attended my games and I wanted to stay reasonably close so they would be able to see me play.

I had wanted to play in the Big Ten Conference, and Illinois seemed to be the right fit for me. The conference was very strong. They played good, solid football and all the teams were well-respected by other teams in conferences around the country. The head coach at Illinois was Bob Blackman. He was there my entire five years, though he was let go after my senior season. He was a nice man who went back to the Ivy Leagues after he left Illinois. He put together a pretty good staff that related very well to the players.

I lived in the dorm with Brian Diedrich, another linebacker on the team. Two other players who lived kitty-corner from us, Jeff Chrystal and Jack Dombroski, are two of my best friends to this day. Our friendship has lasted all of these years.

I was a freshman at Illinois in 1972, which was the very first year that freshmen were eligible to play on the varsity. We also had a freshman team, so they moved you up and sent you down depending on the varsity's needs. I played special teams on varsity, so it was a good way to get my feet wet. My freshman year we played seven teams that were ranked in the top 10 in the nation. We were a .500 program at best, so it was a tough road. But I was loving the game each week and being a part of the team was pretty special.

In the beginning Illinois saw me as a tight end, but that failed because, frankly, I was not a tight end. Then they wanted me to move to defensive end because I was getting bigger. Eventually I got so big they moved me to defensive tackle. I weighed about 270 pounds—a long way from my weight in early high school. I played my sophomore year at defensive tackle. We didn't have a great team but we were competitive. We were still in the middle of the pack. At that time the only bowl game we were eligible to compete in was the Rose Bowl, and that just wasn't feasible for us.

Pro football wasn't even on my radar at the time. We watched the Chicago Bears and St. Louis Cardinals, but I didn't give a lot of thought to a pro career during my early years at Illinois. I tore up my knee (MCL) during my sophomore season in the spring football game. I had surgery and had to sit out a year, which turned out to be a blessing in disguise. When I came back, they gave me the opportunity to move back to linebacker. I guess I can say that my knee injury was a key to my success.

Sitting out the full season I lost all the extra weight I had put on and got myself in shape to play football. I was down to about 235 pounds, perfect for a linebacker, and the rest is history. Going into my senior season, the notion of playing professional football became more of a possibility. We talked about it a lot during the season; our coaches were a big help to me in that regard. I had established myself as a middle linebacker and was having a good season. *Football, football, football* was about all I could think about. I was living in a small bubble.

I really enjoyed college football. I loved to play. I loved Saturdays in the fall. I don't have a lot of standout memories, but I do remember the one and only touchdown I scored. It was at Iowa, and I turned an interception into a touchdown. In all my high school years, my college years, and 14 years of pro football, that's the only time I ever found the end zone. I think it was about 30 yards to the goal line, a memory etched in my mind forever. (Although when I go over it in my mind, the race keeps getting longer, something like 70 yards or so!) It was a sprint to the end zone like no other; I was not going to be denied.

There were two men in particular during my college career who helped me. Gary Golden was the defensive coordinator at Illinois and really cared about his players. Our linebacker coach was Dave Adolph, and he had been around the Big Ten Conference for a long time. Both of them were very intense, and I fed off of their energy. I had the passion, as I said before, but they were the kind of guys you never wanted to let down. They were also accessible; I could go and talk to them about anything. Having that kind of a relationship with them fed into my own drive. They genuinely cared about us players and their passion and enthusiasm rubbed off on me to the highest degree.

I finished college football with a lot of hope. More than anything, I wanted to play football professionally. Football then was a lot different than it is today. Now there is so much press, notoriety, and coverage that just wasn't there when I was playing. Today the media and scouts start to talk about these kids as soon as they enter college, and in some cases while they are still in high school. Players in my time couldn't come out early for the NFL Draft; you had to wait until your senior season was over and then prepare for the draft. And there was only local reporting on potential draftees, not nearly the fanfare that there is today.

Before the draft I played in several postseason football games. I played in the East-West Shrine Game, the Hula Bowl, and then I went to the Japan Bowl, all in three weeks' time. It was a long three weeks but I enjoyed every minute of it. There was no NFL Combine back then either, so I had about three or four workouts with some of the teams before the draft and that was it. I wasn't even sure some teams knew I existed. That troubled me somewhat, but I was eager and ready to get drafted. I worked out as much as I could to keep myself in shape waiting for the draft to come.

The NFL had twelve rounds in the draft spanning two days, and I certainly was not one of the elite players huddled in New York waiting to be picked. There was a lot of mystery. I didn't know what was going to happen. There were no cell phones back then, so guys had to sit by the phone all day waiting for that one phone call from a team telling them that they'd been drafted.

I sat by my phone all day on the draft's first day and never got a call. It was extremely frustrating and very disappointing. My parents would call to see what was going on and all I could say was, "I gotta go. I gotta get off the phone in case someone calls." But no one called.

After not hearing anything on that first day I was really discouraged. I thought I would go in the fourth or maybe the fifth round. I guess my expectations were too high. My roommates and I went downtown in Champaign and tried to celebrate a little bit. I don't know what in the world we were celebrating, but we had a little fun anyway. Anything to get our minds off things for a while. You play your four years of college football and then you sit by the phone all day hoping a team will call you and say that they want you. It's just nuts.

The next day, it was the same thing: wait by the phone and hope it rings. Finally, into the afternoon, I got the call. It was the football administrative assistant at the Minnesota Vikings calling. I remember what she said to her last word: "This is Patti Crowe of the Minnesota Vikings and we have selected you in the ninth round and will see you in August." That was it. I didn't talk to a coach, the general manager, or even a ball boy. It took about 30 seconds if that, but I was ecstatic. I was drafted by the Minnesota Vikings! I didn't think they even knew I existed. But they must have, because I got drafted by them!

I hadn't been a Vikings fan. I didn't pay a lot of attention to their players and knew little about the team, but I was pumped and ready to go. The guys and I turned around and went back out. Now we really did have something to celebrate. I was a Minnesota Viking!

It was a tremendous relief. There were not any minicamps back then, so the first time I came to Minnesota was the day before we had to report. I had signed a contract sometime during the summer, and the guy who negotiated the contract was Frank Gilliam, a former football player and front-office administrator for the Vikings. I called Frank from a pay phone and we settled on $22,000 for the first year, $24,000 for the second year, and a signing bonus of $4,000, which was a lot of money back then. I was happy with the contract and ready to play pro football. I was going to get paid to play a game I loved. It was a very special feeling and hard to believe, but I had never been more ready for anything.

CHAPTER TWO

Training Camp

The night before training camp began, players reported to the Holiday Inn right near the old Metropolitan Stadium. We checked in for one night, and then went off to Mankato the next day in buses. I'd never even been to the Vikings' offices at that point. My roommate on that first night was Tommy Kramer, and he would be from then on. We hit it off immediately and remain friends to this day. It didn't take very long for me to see what a great quarterback Tommy was. He had it all. And of course he was an exceptional player for the Minnesota Vikings for many years.

Under Bud Grant, we were typically the last team in the league to report to training camp. One of the things I learned early on with Bud is you always knew what to expect. We knew what the NFL schedule was and we knew what Bud's schedule was. I'm not sure why we reported so late to camp. It may have been that Bud disliked training camp just as much as everyone else did.

Typically, once my football season ended I would take maybe a week off and then go right back to training again. Keeping in shape was very important to me. So when training camp began my first year, I was ready. Still, that first year in Minnesota was very different. I didn't know if I was going to make the team. I didn't know *anything*. In college, I knew I was on the team—I never had a doubt. But the pros? Well, I was concerned. For one thing, the Vikings had played in the Super Bowl the year before, and they had a strong veteran football team coming into the season.

It seemed as if I had just left the Illinois campus, and suddenly there I was at training camp with the Minnesota Vikings. There were a lot of unknowns waiting for me in Mankato. There were veteran players all over the place. The linebackers were a healthy and strong veteran group—Wally Hilgenberg, Amos Martin, Fred McNeill, Matt Blair, Jeff Siemon, and me. (Roy Winston had just retired.) About halfway through camp, I started to feel a little more comfortable that I could play with these guys. I seemed to be big enough and fast enough, and I established early on that I could hit people. I was beginning to fit in—at least somewhat.

Our first preseason game was against the Los Angeles Rams in Los Angeles. We had about 20 rookies on the team, and I recall Bud telling us that we were all going to play and to be ready. Well, the game happened and not a single one of us got any playing time. That was one of the ways that Bud let you know that he was in control. I mean, not one of us played a down the entire game!

The next game we were at home. I was on the special teams and got into the game. First thing, we kicked off and I ran down the field and knocked down the Browns' entire wedge. I destroyed it—and almost myself in the process. I hurt my arm, my ankle…I can't recall what *didn't* hurt. I gutted my way through the first half and then was out for the rest of the game. Luckily I recovered soon after. At the moment of the collision, though, I wasn't sure if I was ever going to play again. I felt pain like never before.

About midway through camp, they let the guy go who was playing behind Jeff Siemon, and because I was the third guy, I took it as a promising sign. One day I was having a really bad day and Jocko Nelson, who was the linebackers coach, came up to me at practice and told me to settle down and relax. He told me I was going to make the football team. I've always appreciated that because it did settle me down. It was a tremendous relief. I had been pretty nervous about making the cut, but after that conversation with Jocko, it seemed like things got a lot easier. Bud never talked to me about it. In fact, he never said a word to me the entire training camp. Not one single word. Well, *once*. I'll mention that later.

I did not follow the Vikings growing up and had not heard much about Bud. He was so stoic—guarded, you could say. But I did learn one thing quickly: when Bud did say something, it always made sense. He was not a big talker, but if he looked at you the wrong way, it would melt your heart and scare you half to death. He had a command and a presence about him that demanded attention. He was no-nonsense. When he came into the room and got in front of the team, you had better be listening. He has not changed one bit in all the years that I have known him.

There were a few veterans on the team who controlled the locker room, and Bud controlled them. It was just that simple. Jim Marshall was the premier leader of the team. He was very vocal and a real stand-up guy. There were multiple leaders on the team. Fran Tarkenton played the last two years of his career with me. The famous

Purple People Eaters were there: Marshall, Carl Eller, and Alan Page. There were others too—Paul Krause, Ahmad Rashad, Sammy White, Stu Voigt, Ron Yary, Ed White, Chuck Foreman, and so many more.

The team had been in the Super Bowl the year before and was full of guys who had been there forever. This was a seasoned, veteran football team. The bulk of the players had been together for over a decade. But even among all of those great players, there was no doubt who was in charge: Bud Grant. Every single thing on this football team was done Bud's way, not a doubt from anyone.

What I remember the most about training camp was there was no water on the field. We had one water break and that was dependent on Bud, whenever he saw fit to have it. Bud had some things he did that were different. We lined up for the national anthem, even in practice sessions, years before the league started it. Bud also had the infamous bat drill. You would run a distance, put down a bat, run around it several times, and then return. By the end you would be dizzy as hell. It was good for some fun as long as you weren't the one on the bat drill. Bud had his way of doing things. I thought then that Bud did those kinds of things to let you know who was in charge, but he never had to do any of them. We all knew.

During the off-season there was no schedule for weight lifting or working out, but it was expected that players keep in shape and come to camp in good shape. Still I felt like a lot of the veterans used training camp to get in shape for the season. I know some of the guys didn't work out at all until June, with camp just a few weeks away. I took hardly any break. I ran and lifted weights almost all year long. I would run sprints and jog and did just about everything I could to stay in shape. I recall going out to Lake Calhoun and running around the lake, trying to do it in under 21 minutes. It was what I used as a measuring stick as to my football conditioning. We did things on our own. The Vikings did not have a strength coach. Fred Zamberletti was the trainer, Stubby Eason was the equipment guy, and that was it. Most of the players had their own training routines.

The game was not by any means as complicated as it is today. I knew I could compete. The game was smaller and slower and not as detailed. There were not as many facets to it; it was not as specialized. We had just a few blitz packages and coverage schemes. Now, I'm not saying that I couldn't have played in today's game, but it was not the same.

Everyone liked running the football. The size of players was much different too. Mick Tingelhoff, our center, was probably 265 pounds and Ed White, who was one of the biggest guys, was about 285 to 290 pounds. That's nothing compared to today, where 300 pounds or more is commonplace. When I played I weighed about 235 pounds, my college weight. I believe that I was faster than what they thought I was. Stu Voigt, a great tight end for us, once quipped about himself, "Our opponents had me down as a player with deceptive speed: slower than we thought."

Tommy Kramer and I were two of the rookies that made it that season. Bud was not a proponent of keeping rookies around, but the first year I was there five rookies made the team. We had a great group of guys. Jerry Burns was our offensive coordinator, and I will say he is the same guy today as he was way back then. Burnsie was a great football coach with a tremendous mind for the offensive side of the ball. He was very beloved by everyone and is one of the funniest guys I have ever known.

The veterans on the Vikings were very good to the young guys. On both sides of the ball, they really got along well with the rookies. We were in training camp for six weeks, with twice-daily practices, so we spent a lot of time together. Once you showed them you could compete, I think the veterans realized that some of us rookies could help them win, and that's all it took. I was always impressed with the way we were treated. It was nice to be accepted by the majority of the veteran guys, especially since they had been together for so long.

Jeff Siemon was the starting middle linebacker during my first season, and he was a great player and an exceptional person. He had been a Pro Bowl guy and remained there for a few years after I arrived. I started to work my way into the rotation the first year and actually started two games when Jeff was hurt. Getting hurt was the toughest part of the game. Our Hall of Fame center, Mick Tingelhoff, never got hurt. Mick was as tough as it gets, and his durability is legendary. There was a story about the backup center in the early 1970s on the Vikings, Godfrey Zaunbrecher. He once said, "I'm the third team center on a team with only two centers. I play behind Mick Tingelhoff and Tingelhoff hurt."

I always had those I looked up to when playing. When I was at the University of Illinois, Bob Blackman brought an Ivy League mentality to the game. He had a good staff around him. Dave Adolph, who I mentioned before, was the linebackers coach and was a great mentor to me while I was there. With the pros I spent a lot of time with Jeff Siemon and Wally Hilgenberg, both of whom mentored me. Matt Blair was always open and very helpful to me. People like Jim Marshall and Paul Krause were also the consummate pro football players, and I learned so much by just being around them. I was very fortunate to have people like that at both the collegiate level and at the professional level.

In 1977 we won the division championship and got into the play-offs. We got to the conference finals and lost to Dallas in the NFC Championship Game. I was thinking to myself, *Wow, this is pretty sweet. We went to the championship game my first year. We're going to do this every year. What a great time this is going to be.* Well, we didn't get there again until my 10th season. People just don't realize how hard it is.

In my second year, I lost my way somewhat. I wasn't playing well and just couldn't get going. Looking back, it may have been that I was overconfident, maybe a little too full of myself. What snapped me out of it was they brought in a guy for me to work out with. I couldn't understand what they were doing, but Bud told me to work out with this guy. *Why would they want me to work out with this guy?* It didn't make any sense to me. I think it was Bud checking up on me. So I did it, and worked my way through my issues. Bud had some kind of a strategy, I guess. A short time later the guy was cut from the team. I guess it was just Bud's way of telling me that there was always going to be someone around to take my place. And it worked, because I snapped out of it pretty darn fast.

I played a lot on special teams, almost all of them. I was starting to play pretty regularly by my third year and became a regular starter in my fourth season. It felt great. My career was taking off and I loved every minute of it. My dream was being fulfilled.

Tommy Kramer started a few games early on when Fran was hurt, and then once Fran retired Tommy started for the next 10 years. Tommy was an exceptional player. He was extremely intelligent, had a great arm and a keen sense for the game. He could make all the throws. He was the premier quarterback for us.

There were so many guys around me who were so good. Matt Blair was a great player for the Vikings for so many years. Here was a guy that was six foot six inches tall and weighed about 235 pounds and could run and jump, make tackles, and block kicks. He was just fun to watch, such a great player. He blocked so many kicks in his career, more than most other teams combined. You could model your game after Matt. He was so prepared and worked so hard at his craft. I was very sad to hear that he had been so sick and passed on recently.

I was very serious about the game, and as a result I got along with everyone. I am very proud of the tremendous work ethic that I brought with me to high school, college, and to the Vikings. I have always been extremely competitive, passionate, and always gave everything I had on the football field. I always felt like I could play forever—and I almost did.

CHAPTER THREE

A Vikings Regular

Playing linebacker in the NFL was much different from college football, no question about it. The game was bigger, faster, and more
athletic…but still nothing like it is today. To me, it was the epitome of
football competition. And I was there right in the middle of it.

Week in and week out you had to establish yourself as a bona fide
starter in the National Football League; you had to establish yourself
as a 16-game regular. Every week you were not just putting your job
on the line or your career on the line, you were putting your future on
the line. You were putting your face out there as a starting player on
the Minnesota Vikings.

It was always important to be a guy that you could count on. Bud
always preached about dependability, reliability, and durability. You
had to be a guy that he could count on week in and week out. I learned
a lot about this from the older players on the team. I counted on those
guys to teach me.

There were some great players in the NFL who were my significant
competition. There is no question that the guy at the top of that list

is Walter Payton of the Chicago Bears. He was one of those guys that always brought his A game; he brought his competitiveness to you on every single play. He could run and catch the ball. Walter was an unbelievable talent who was so driven and so focused. He was almost too much of a nice guy as a person—but he never played like that nice guy. He was in a class by himself. He was at the top of the heap—especially when it came to setting an unbelievably high standard.

As a defense, we didn't pay attention to the other teams' defensemen. Our focus was on stopping the offense. *How are we going to stop their scheme?* That was our daily focus. We got really locked in specifics like, *What are we going to do to stop Jerry Rice of the 49ers? What can we do to stop Sterling Sharpe? What can we do to make life problematic for Joe Montana? How are we going to keep these guys from beating us?*

Our defense was based on schematics and what the tendencies were that people would exhibit during certain setups. It was very much situational football as opposed to the way it is today. Back then teams would try to establish the ground game and then throw when they had to. Today, throwing the ball is much more common. We made a living between our defensive ends because that's where all the action was. It was run first. Today it is almost the exact opposite.

When I signed on with the Vikings I really didn't know what to expect, but I did know one thing: they knew how to win. In fact, they won almost all of the time. Winning was commonplace. They had been to three recent Super Bowls, won many division titles, and were an exceptional, well-established football team. They had a great record in the few seasons prior to my arrival.

The coaching staff was very small. We had four guys who coached the defense and also helped out on special teams. The game was much simpler all around. Take our schedules, for instance. Once the regular season started, we would go in on Mondays at noon. We were typically out of there by 5:00 at the latest. Today it is all day, every day. Quite simply, Bud ran a tight ship. He never wasted any time. Bud always had a laser focus. When he was on the football field, he was all football. When he was with his family, he was all family. When he was hunting, he was all hunting.

He would never schedule practice on a Saturday until late in the day because he would go hunting first. He would bring his dog with him into the locker room when he got there and that's just the way it was. We understood it. We accepted it.

I was known for my work ethic, something that makes me very proud. I worked out with weights before most teams even had weight rooms. Luckily for me, I grew fast and put on my weight in high school. I mean, I put on a hundred pounds and grew a foot!

I quietly looked up to my brother. We were always trying to get one leg up on the other and it developed for us a competitive approach to everything we did. This set the tone for me and made me really stretch my abilities. In high school our competition kept us somewhat at odds with each other, but then when he went off to college things changed and we became great friends as well as brothers. He's a really good guy, a great competitor, and we are still close today.

I would never say I was a top-notch athlete, but I would consider myself an athlete who had some compensating factors—my work ethic, instincts, and my passion for the game. I absolutely loved playing football. I tried other sports too. But I wasn't any good at basketball. It was the same with wrestling too. But then I got interested in lifting weights. I started out in the garage at home. I moved on to the YMCA and then to a place called the Pit and continued my weight lifting. I really enjoyed it.

I learned from an early age that if you wanted to participate in competitive sports, you had to work at it. I faced an uphill battle from the beginning because I was so small. Once I started growing I got more confidence. I got stronger and bigger and faster. And when you put together my size and instincts, I knew that I had a chance to be successful in the long term.

As a pro, I worked out mostly during the off-season. In season, when we were done with practice on a given day, it was tough to then go off to another facility to lift weights. We didn't have a facility at the Vikings complex, so I went to a Lifetime Fitness facility close by when I could. At the old Metropolitan Stadium we had a few free weights and a universal machine, and no one ever really used them much. Bud was not a believer in lifting weights. I think he felt like it was a waste of time. One day he walked by me when I was lifting weights at Winter Park and said, "Why don't you just go home and shovel some snow?" That's the way he was—and he was serious. He really thought I would get just as good of a workout by shoveling.

During the off-season I had a regular routine of lifting. I think I lost some strength and conditioning during the season because I was doing different kinds of things with my body and lifting less frequently. I did weights, the elliptical machines, and the stair climbers. I enjoyed doing it. It wasn't difficult and I didn't dread it by any means. Actually, it was inspiring for me.

We didn't have the regimented workouts until later in my career. Our routine got a little more advanced starting around the mid-1980s. They brought in strength coaches for in-season and off-season training, and I fell right into that. I always thought it was a good thing to keep my body in great shape all season long.

When I started out playing for the Vikings I was on many of the special teams. Early in my career, I was the guy right next to the kicker on kickoffs, on the front line on the kick return team, and a guard on the punt team. I was not on the field goal team or the extra-point team. I enjoyed being on special teams, as it was a way to get on the field. It is one of the reasons that I rarely sat down during a game. When you are off the field, there are always sudden changes; it kept me engaged and kept me interested. Plus, I didn't want to sit on the bench. I was too wound up to sit down and take a break. I was ready to go all the time.

Once I became a starter I was more of a special teams backup, but I was a personal protector on the punt teams forever. The personal protector is the last line of defense. You set the front and make the calls and keep the punt from getting blocked. I was on that team until my final game in the NFL. I had only one punt come close to being blocked. I kind of whiffed on Reggie White when he was in Green Bay. Frankly, he just kind of ran me over—but he didn't block the kick. I blocked a kick once. It was a punt, during a playoff game in my second season—the game when we went out to Los Angeles and beat the Rams before losing to Dallas in the championship game.

As I said before, when I was playing, I was the middle linebacker, and my job was to make the calls in the huddle and at the line of scrimmage. We would huddle up and I would make the call whether it was a bear front or an over front or an under front or a 4-3 front or whatever the call may be. It basically directs the defensive linemen about where they are going to go. The linebackers already know where they are going to go based on the front. And then you make the coverage call. It sounds like a lot and very complicated but it really wasn't.

Once the offense comes up to the ball, you identify the strength of the formation, you identify where the receivers are, you identify the set for the backfield, and then if you have to make changes you check it, change it, or keep it as is. In addition, when the offense comes up to the ball and lines up in a formation for which the coverage has to change, you change it. It is just that simple—and I'm sure all of the readers know exactly what calls were made. Right?

The defensive coordinator would signal the play call, but depending on what the offense was doing, changes had to be made. A lot of the checks that we made were pretty universal. We would change the play call, you had to be sure that everyone was on the same page. Still with me? The coaches would tweak the game plans based on the tendencies of the opposing team and you had to communicate every snap.

I really enjoyed setting the defense. The longer you are in the league, the mental part of the game becomes much easier. Because of experience you understand the game and are in a better position to make the necessary calls.

You also study the tendencies of the other teams. Our coaching staff did a great job of preparing you for each team that we would face on Sunday. There are always some tweaks and different looks week in and week out, but for the most part, if you do your homework, you are ready for game day.

Typically we would go back and look at the opposing team's three previous games to see what they were the most likely to do by down and distance or formation. We looked at what they had done in the past and try to figure out what they might do to attack us. It was a challenge and somewhat of a chess match.

The game is more complicated today than when I played, but you still had to know what people were doing, anticipate their tendencies, and make game day adjustments. The mental part of it was very important and was a big part of my job.

I put in the time. I would go in on Tuesdays, which actually was our day off, and watch film and talk to the coaches. Tuesday was a very busy day for the coaches, so I didn't take up too much of their time on that day, but I did watch film. I also tried to spend time with my family on those days off, even though my mind was preoccupied. A lot of the time the teams in our division were fairly predictable. We found that they didn't do a lot of things differently when we played them the second time.

For teams that had the great runners, we knew that those guys were going to touch the ball 20 to 25 times a game, so that's what we had to prepare for when we studied the tape. It was the teams that mixed things up and would go against their tendencies that were always a challenge. The teams that started to go with three and four wide receivers created matchup problems. San Francisco was very good at that tactical part of the game; they would also mix and match with their personnel to complicate things and distract your keys and reads.

The Lions were a team that tended to throw the ball a little more—until they got Barry Sanders. Once he came into the league, if you didn't get the ball to him most of the time, then you ought to be ashamed of yourself and might be looking for a job. The same held true with Chicago and Walter Payton. You knew in order to beat them you were going to have to stop the ground game. The Packers were not as talented during my playing years, but the rivalry was still strong. You never knew what the outcome of those games was going to be.

Once I became a regular player, I was counted on for many things. As a middle linebacker, I had to set the huddle, call the plays, had to make the checks, and basically run the show on defense. The nature of the position just demanded it. Back then the middle linebacker was the focal point of the defense. I had to sharpen my communication skills. That was probably the biggest adjustment for me.

We had a lot of guys on defense who had been in the league for a long time. I had to earn their respect. I didn't have a problem with that because I knew that it was a part of my job on offense. Mick Tingelhoff was one of the best of them. He was a great guy, a wily veteran. I had a great deal of respect for him. He was a crusty old player who wasn't very big—certainly by today's standards, anyway—but he was so smart. He was so durable and reliable.

My first year in training camp, I recall him chasing me and telling me to slow down. Mick was a lunch-bucket guy. He came to work and did his job—and he did it so well for 17 seasons. He was so unique, extremely tough, never got hurt. He was just there…all the time. He was certainly one of Bud's kind of guys. He commanded the respect of his teammates because he earned it. He was also a family man and such a nice guy.

Fran Tarkenton was with us for two years during my career. Francis was extremely smart and very talented, very tough, very resilient. He had a great mind for the game. He was very private, as I said, and to this day he still is. He would come to work and do his job; then he had his life outside of football that didn't carry over. Still, he was a very approachable guy. He treated rookies the same as everybody else. Francis was always good to me and I appreciated it. I could sit down with him today and talk with him for hours. He was one of the greatest quarterbacks to ever play the game. I believe when he retired he owned every passing record in the National Football League.

I played for 14 years in the National Football League and I never worked another job during the off-season. Working in the off-season was more of a carryover with some of the older players. I was paid $22,000 a season, and that was plenty of money back then. I didn't want to work at anything else. The way I saw it, football was my job, period. I took the off-season to prepare myself for the next one.

There were some big changes for the franchise that happened during my career. In 1982 we moved from playing outside at the old Metropolitan Stadium to playing inside at the Metrodome. I played outside for five years. I loved it outside in all of the elements. I loved every minute of playing at the old Met. It was a great atmosphere, like the one in Green Bay today. There was an intimacy with the fans that was just unbelievable. Sometimes we would go outside and stay out with the fans for hours afterward. I think we lost that when we moved inside. There were some memorable games outside in the cold, rain, and snow. The temperatures could get so low, it would be brutal. But I always felt that was the way football was supposed to be played.

When we moved to the Metrodome, the whole atmosphere felt kind of sterile that first year. The turf wasn't very good either. But it became our home and we got used to it. It did have its advantages. For one thing, it got extremely loud inside. We played the game the same way, but it was just different.

Bud didn't like it at all. He thrived on being outside, cultivating the field and the climate to our advantage. Our durability in the elements was one of our advantages. Bud never let us players use hand warmers or sideline heaters, and I know he loved to see the opposing teams come in and freeze on the sideline during the games. They would be standing there next to the heaters and we would be out there as if it were a beautiful day. And it worked. I never really got cold no matter what the temperature was outside. I suppose I was always too much into the game to even think about it.

Teams would come up from the South or in from the West and we would be standing on the sideline or out on the field while they huddled around heaters trying to keep warm. They were freezing their asses off while we were out there enjoying ourselves. Or at least we thought we were.

Bud never let any of us have any hand warmers but I always wondered, *Did he have some in his pocket?* There were rumors. I don't know, and I sure was not—then or now—going to ask him. For the record, in case Bud is reading this, I never really thought he had any in his pocket.

It was a different era of football. We loved the home-field weather as an advantage. There was a certain mystique about the outdoor conditions, the Vikings, and all that went with it. Once we were inside, the game opened up a little more. The Vikings became an indoor team at a time when the league was opening up to the pass a lot more. The transition from running the football down people's throats to throwing the ball was a significant change in the game, and we were forced to change with it. No longer did teams fear coming to Minnesota because of the weather. I would have preferred to play outside all of the time, but that's me. It was okay to move in, but I do think we lost something when we moved into the dome. Everything was so pristine and clean. I had to get used to it.

Indoors and out, I had a great career with the Vikings. And there are some games that I will never forget. One of the best was during my rookie season, when we won the opening round of the playoffs and advanced to the NFC Championship Game. We went to Dallas, got beat, and then the season was over. At the time I figured, *We'll just do this every year.* But as I said, it was 10 years before we did it again.

The playoff loss to Washington 10 years later was probably the toughest loss of my 14 years with the Vikings. We were playing on the road. It was the 1987 season, the year of the strike. We played the first two games of the regular season and then the strike players took over, losing the next three games. These were players the Vikings picked up from just about anywhere. We then came back to win several games but lost three of the last four, barely backing into the playoffs. But then we got on a roll. We beat the Saints easily and then went out to San Francisco and beat the 49ers, the No. 1 seed in the NFC.

Against Washington, we had a chance to tie it in the last minute but ended up falling 17–10. That game really affected me. It got to me. I broke down in the locker room and cried like a baby. My wife was at the game and she was surprised by my tears. "You didn't cry when we had our babies!" she told me.

What hurt so much was the thought that we might never get back to the championship game again. I didn't realize as a rookie how difficult it was to get that far. The average fan doesn't realize how extremely difficult it is to just get there, let alone win it. I think I played pretty well in that Washington game, but the loss was devastating. It took me a long time to get over it.

As a regular on the Vikings I think I was vocal when I needed to be vocal. I believe I was a leader. I tried to be more of a lead-by-example type of guy. I missed a few games here and there from injuries, broke a few thumbs and fingers and was out for short periods of time, but I was basically a pretty healthy guy. The worst injury I had playing was a torn groin muscle. I missed a few weeks with that. I suffered more injuries and had more surgeries after I was done playing than I ever had while playing. As a player I wanted to be on the field and would have played hurt if they had let me.

CHAPTER FOUR

Some Great Teammates

I was extremely blessed in my 14-year career to play with some exceptional football players. It would not be fair if I didn't recognize these individuals and what they meant to me and the Vikings. The special relationship that I had with these players will impact me for the rest of my life.

One of our all-time great linebackers was Matt Blair. For a guy that was as big as he was—about 6'6" and around 240 pounds—he was an outstanding athlete. He could run and had great extension because of his basketball background. He was very intelligent, a consummate team guy who was really into football and a private person off the field. He was always doing the right thing. I know Bud considered him to be someone he could really depend on. Matt took care of business, blocked a ton of kicks using his long arms and massive frame. We played together for a number of years, well after he established himself as a great linebacker.

The other side of the linebacker crew was Fred McNeil. Fred was also an outstanding athlete who could really run. He had great range and was a good cover guy. He was one of those guys who was always playing, and playing extremely well, another very durable player. He was a very intelligent person who went on to get a law degree. Fred died of ALS disease a few years ago.

Another great linebacker was Wally Hilgenberg. Wally was a really tough guy who seemed like he had played the game forever. He was an Iowa guy, as hard-nosed as they come. He knew the game and had a great feel for the scheme that the Vikings ran. He had a bit of a mean streak in him. Some thought he was a dirty player, but he really wasn't. He just played the game hard. He played to win.

Wally helped me a great deal when I first came into the league. The very first day after my very first practice, he pulled me aside and suggested we go have a beer. What I didn't know is that the beer was a reward for taking him to pick up his truck. Seriously, though, I loved Wally. He was such a nice guy off the field and our friendship lasted until he died, also of ALS, a few years back. I learned a lot about the game from him and he will always remain in my fondest memories.

Gary Zimmerman played center at Oregon, then he came in here in a trade and they stuck him at left tackle. He went on to become one of the best to ever play the game, a Hall of Famer. He was bigger than you thought he was. He was a better athlete than you thought he was too, and he had great body control. He was so strong and could absolutely anchor his position. He played with great feet and had leverage—he could do everything. He was also very intelligent. He had amazing football instincts.

In practice he had to battle every day against Chris Doleman, day in and day out. They made each other better players. Their game days were probably easy for them compared to what they faced each day at practice. Gary had such great control mentally, emotionally, and physically. He rarely was out of position, was never on the ground, and rarely ever beaten. He was just a great player.

One of my best friends on the team, who played with me for many years, was Mark Mullaney. When I first got here, Mark was a backup to Carl Eller and Jim Marshall as kind of a swing player. He had been in the league a couple of years at that point. He had an extensive basketball background and played in college at Colorado State. He was built like a Greek god and could run like a deer. He took his game very seriously and was always working to improve it. He was very dedicated to his craft.

Injuries derailed his career somewhat at the end, but he still had a long, successful tenure. He was a wonderful teammate with a great sense of humor, an easy guy to get along with. My wife and I are very close friends with his family. He has been in the sales business for a long time, though he is now semiretired.

Jeff Siemon was the middle linebacker for the Vikings when I arrived. He was a grown-up playing a kids' game. Jeff was very smart, and an outstanding football player who in my opinion was extremely underrated. Although we didn't run in the same circles, he was always there for me. If I had a question about something, I could always count on Jeff for the answer. He carried himself like a true professional on and off the field. To this day, when I see him we always have a lot to talk about. Although we didn't have a lot in common, we had football in common—and that was as important as anything.

Bobby Bryant was an ornery little cuss. I saw him recently at our alumni get-together. He is a funny guy, brutally honest, and was one heck of a football player. He was a defensive back who could make all the plays. He was never exceptionally fast but somehow he got the job done. He made some spectacular plays for us over the years. He had great cover instincts and was a great zone corner. He had tremendous feel for the game and was an exceptional teammate.

Anthony Carter had so many incredible skills as a wide receiver. His talent was tremendous, though if you looked at his Combine skills today, he might not fare very well. He wasn't very big or strong, and he wasn't fast as receivers went, but he could make plays. He could return punts and kicks and was fearless. He had great instincts and could get open. He was a gamer and I enjoyed being on the team with him. He was just a great player, plain and simple. Jerry Burns, our head football coach at the time, loved Anthony because he was tougher than nails. He was reliable and could catch the ball anywhere on the field and then really run with it. He played so far above and beyond his skill set.

Dave Casper was only with us for one year. He came from the Houston Oilers and was one of the best tight ends to ever play the game. But here, he drew a No. 44 and was asked to play guard for us during the Steckel year, which went over like a ton of bricks. I always wondered how you could ask a guy who was one of the best tight ends ever to play the game to play on the offensive line, but it wasn't my decision, so I kept quiet. Dave was a real character. He had great ball skills and was a really hard-nosed football player. He was a little overweight when he came in and we were all rather shocked when he drew his number. It did not sit well with him either. I thought he was a great guy, a very smart player, and I always enjoy seeing him.

Fred Cox was the first player I met when I joined the Vikings. When I got to the old Holiday Inn, which is now the Mall of America,

Fred was standing at the front desk. I got into the hotel and looked at him and thought to myself, *Well, maybe I've got a chance here.* Fred didn't quite have the build of a football player. He was a quiet guy, studious. He did so many things to help the Vikings. Bud had him doing all kinds of things at practice. Fred was not a gym rat—he was no Adonis—but he had a great career with Minnesota. He was a very reliable kicker, extremely dependable—Bud's kind of guy.

D.J. Dozier was a very nice person, a good locker room guy. He did his job and kept to himself quite a bit. I never got to know him very well but always thought that he was a good football player and a quality person.

The one thing these guys have in common is I liked every one of them. I always felt that I was lucky to play the game for as long as I did, and am especially grateful for all of the friendships that I have made. My teammates have always meant the world to me. I may miss a few here but I will never forget any of them.

Jim Hough was an extremely strong man. He was an exceptionally hard worker. When Jim got his hands on you, he could move you. He was a quiet human being who just went about his business. We trained a lot together in the off-season. Jim and I were also in the NFL arm wrestling championships together. Every NFL team had two guys in the competition, a heavyweight and a lightweight. Jim was the heavyweight and I was the lightweight. But the first year Jim hurt his arm, so I went into that division too and ended up winning both. (More about that a little later.)

Tim Irwin was a really, really good football player. By today's standards he may not have been considered a great athlete, but he was special. He was extremely strong, extraordinarily smart, a great worker, and very competitive. He played for a long time with the Vikings at a very high level. He got the most out of his skill set. He came to work every day, competed like hell in practice, and was tenacious. He was a very prideful person. He was also a very fun person to be around. He saw himself as a country singer and liked to perform. Today he works in Tennessee as a juvenile court judge.

Archie Manning came to us from New Orleans during Bud's last year and stayed with us for Steckel's year. He was at the tail end of his career when he came to Minnesota. He was a very likable guy who did a tremendous job raising three boys, two of whom became great NFL quarterbacks. He was very humble and respectful, a very unassuming guy. He was just an all-around nice person.

I will never forget that game against the Bears in Chicago in 1984. I can honestly say I have never seen a player take a beating like he took in that game. He was sacked 11 times. I mean, the Bears absolutely killed Archie. They just beat the hell out of him over and over, play after play. He retired soon after he left the Vikings, and I don't blame him after the way he was treated that day in Chicago.

When I first met Jim Marshall, he was the oldest player on the team and I was one of the youngest. He was the unquestioned leader. When Bud wanted something done or wanted something said, he had Jim do it. The loyalty between Bud and Jim was as strong as anything I've seen; they had so much mutual respect. Jim was not a very big player, but he could sure run. I think he could still chase down one of those scat backs of today. What a football player he was. He was and will always be Captain Jim.

He was very intelligent and he was very adventurous, a little on the wild side—a real character. To have played as long as he did without ever missing a game was unbelievable. In my opinion, that in and of itself should place him in the Pro Football Hall of Fame. I think he has been done a tremendous disservice not to have even been considered.

As good a player as Carl Eller was, I will say he had the body. Carl was just chiseled. I mean it was almost as if he were carved out of stone. Carl had it all—great strength and ability. I don't think that players, including me, really realized how good Carl was until later on in our careers. He was a giant of a man who could really play football.

Both Marshall and Eller were dominant players who were relentless on game day. They were tough as nails, highly competitive, and were all about football Sunday. They both had great survival skills and relied on their instincts. They played like their hair was on fire all the time.

Alan Page was another one like Carl and Jim. My first year, he came to training camp really late because he was in law school. He also had gotten into long-distance running and came in at about 230 pounds, pretty light for a defensive lineman. I wasn't around to experience Alan at his finest. When I arrived on the scene I found a very intelligent player who was in the closing moments of an incredible career. He played with such great instinct.

I don't think there is any doubt that he will go down as one of the greatest Vikings ever. He was the first player to receive the NFL Player of the Year Award as a defensive player. His career really took off after football and he made it all the way to the Minnesota Supreme Court, where he served honorably until retirement a few years ago. I always thought Alan was a little like Fran Tarkenton in some ways because he had other things going outside of football that were important in his life. Good for them. I respect them for what they did on and off the field.

Doug Martin was an interesting guy, a No. 1 pick for us. He was a strong, agile athlete, a very good player who had a small circle of friends. He was very quick and athletic and had many good years. He played defensive end and anchored the position very well.

One of the greatest receivers I have ever seen on a football field was Ahmad Rashad, aka Bobby Moore. Fran said he was the greatest receiver he had ever seen after just throwing the ball to him in practice and before he ever played a down for us. There was some controversy around an undisclosed injury, but Fran insisted that the Vikings keep him, and the rest is history.

Ahmad was a great athlete. He came into the league as a running back, but he was very graceful and had phenomenal hands, which made him a natural wide receiver. He was so fluid, just an absolute joy to watch. He was not as physical a player as some were, but he was not afraid to mix it up either.

You really can't say much about Ahmad without bringing up the 1980 Cleveland game where he caught the touchdown pass on the last play of the game. I thought the game was over, and then Ahmad made the great catch from Tommy Kramer at the very end and got us into the playoffs. He was an exceptional player and I consider him a very close friend. We have a lot of respect for each other. He was so smart. He has an infectious personality and can blend in with just about any group of people.

Sammy White was the polar opposite of Ahmad. He was exceptionally quiet and wouldn't say boo if he had to. He was a very unassuming person who was extremely tough. He took some tremendous hits catching the ball in heavy traffic and he had incredible ball skills. He was a very nice person who loved to laugh and have a good time. Sammy was a blend-in player. You knew he was always there but he never drew attention to himself. He was the typical player for Bud who just came to work every day and did his job. Bud thought a lot of him.

I played with Chris Doleman for six years and was so saddened when I heard of his passing. He was a really good guy. He had those rare physical traits that made him an exceptional football player. He could run like a deer, he was tall, and he was built as if he had been lifting weights his whole life. He came in as a linebacker but was switched to defensive end. That was great for all of us linebackers because we got sick of him beating on us all the time. Also, defensive end was a natural fit for him because of our scheme at the time and the way the Vikings used him.

He wasn't loud or boisterous, but whenever he was in the room, you just knew he was there. He just had a presence about him that was special. In some ways he reminded me of Fran Tarkenton in that football was his business. He treated it like a business. He came to work every day and did all of the things he needed to do to be successful. Chris liked what football did for him financially, and that was just fine. He had a great career as a Ring of Honor guy and a Hall of Famer. He accomplished everything he set out to do and more. He was just a great person, and I miss him.

Stu Voigt was the prototypical lunch-pail guy. He was a tough, hard-nosed player who had exceptional ball skills. He wasn't real flashy but he came to work every day and did the job for us. He was a great blocker and a tremendous physical player who had a lot of intelligence, a solid tight end. He earned his check every single day. He took care of business as a behind-the-scenes type and never really got the notoriety that he deserved. It was always Bud's thing to have players that were durable, dependable, and reliable and that was Stu to a *T*.

Tommy Kramer and I were roommates forever and remain great friends. We came in as rookies together and lived in a couple different houses in Lakeville. He was a real fun character and a great football player. We probably were not good for each other in our pre-married years, admittedly. If he stayed healthy and had taken better care of himself he probably could have played for 20 years or more.

Tommy had a great feel for the game and unbelievable instincts. The game came easy for him. He used his incredible competitiveness to excel at everything he did, whether it was football, pool, or golf. He may be a little bit underrated but he put up huge numbers as a quarterback. Tommy was so gifted. It's too bad that his career didn't end up what it could have been.

I played only a few years with Chuck Foreman but admired his tremendous skills as a big running back. When I came in he was close to the end of his career, but he still had some great years with the Vikings. He had tremendous vision, with great balance and body control. He played a lot faster than he ever ran. He could do it all—run, catch, block, and make you miss. He had a complete game. He was also very approachable for a veteran player.

Steve Riley played left tackle for us and was a very steady player. He was seemingly held together with tape and glue from all the beatings he took. He was a consistent player who was somewhat underweight. He was a quiet guy, very likable, and an extremely hard worker. He was also a very good technician of the game.

Tommy Hannon was a great defensive back for us and he played for a long time. He was one of five from my draft class who made it.

He was very dependable, a zone safety who had the ability to cover all of the other receivers.

Randy Holloway came to us as a No. 1 draft choice at defensive end. He had some great moments in his career and did a good job for us, although he didn't play that long. Randy was a very likable individual who rarely drew attention to himself. He was one of those guys who could laugh at himself.

Keith Millard was a loud, boisterous, outgoing guy who was an exceptional player. Keith has a great heart, but as a player he had a very short fuse. He was a very passionate player. I could always tell the type of day we were going to have as soon as he came through the door. He was exceptionally strong and had great first-step quickness. There are probably some coaches who would say he was a volatile player and difficult to coach, but on Sunday he always gave it his all. He became a tremendous player in the league for a long time and then went into coaching. Keith is just an all-around good person. I really enjoy it when we can spend some time together.

Carl Lee was another defensive back who played for the Vikings for a long time. Floyd Peters, who came in as our defensive coordinator, was primarily a man-to-man-coverage coach and Carl was a man-to-man-coverage corner. He was so good at man coverage that he allowed us, along with Reggie Rutland, to play out that scheme. He could run with anyone in the league. He had a great temperament for the position and a great feel for the game. To this day, Carl looks like he could still play. He is a good friend.

Reggie Rutland was the flip side to Carl. He went about his business and stayed quiet. He had a three- or four-year window where he played some great football for us. He was one of those guys you could always rely on to be there. Later, he changed his name to Najee Mustafaa. He was a very good athlete and a very good player for the Vikings.

One of my very dear friends on our roster was Keith Nord. I always felt like he was kind of my little brother. He was a walk-on player. He didn't have a snowball's chance in hell of making our football team and yet he stuck around for seven years. I don't think he ever was a starting player, but he did it all on special teams and was always there where the Vikings needed him.

Keith outworked everybody. He was tougher than hell. He was very smart, tremendously fearless, and a great player on our special teams. He was Bud's kind of guy, no question about that. He was one of those players: you knew what you were going to get from him every day. He would get in a lot of fights in practice, had that chip on his shoulder, and it served him well.

When he retired he got into public speaking and was doing very well for himself. One day Dennis Ryan, our equipment guy, came and told me that Keith was very ill. I called him and he called back, but we missed each other. I was scouting in Michigan and called him again and left a message. His wife called me back and told me that he had passed away that morning. Keith's death had a very profound effect on me. In fact, my decision to retire became a no-brainer after that. He had a zest for life like no one I have ever known.

Joe Senser was a great athlete with good ball skills who had his career cut short by knee injuries. He was a very positive, outgoing player. He had everything in the world going for him and he was dealt a really tough hand. Since he retired he has had two strokes and is having a tough time recovering.

Ron Yary was a great player and a Hall of Famer. He was as steady as they come as a right tackle for us. He had great durability. He kind of kept to himself and was a tough, determined player who took his craft very seriously. Once he walked off the field, he went his separate way. I never really got to know him very well but if I ever ran into him I know we could talk for a long time. He was that kind of guy.

One of the best tight ends we ever had with the Vikings was Steve Jordan. He was a tireless worker. He was one of those players who had goals set for himself and met every one of them. He could be somewhat vocal but really led by example. I had a lot of respect for him and I would hope that he would say the same thing about me.

Steve was the player representative for the union. I viewed him as a union guy while I was always the company guy. We differed on some things, but for the most part got along very well. He had a great career and I always thought that at some point he should have been nominated for the Hall of Fame. His numbers and the years he played should certainly earn him consideration.

One of my best friends on the team was Mike Mularkey. Mike has been in this league as a player and coach for many years and he has been a head coach a number of times. For as much time as he has spent in the league I always sort of questioned whether he even liked football. I mean that more tongue in cheek than anything, but I was kind of surprised he went into the coaching business. There was no lack of toughness in him. He was another of the "good guys," fun to be around and a good friend.

One of the funniest guys I have ever known is Rickey Young. He was an unbelievable character, and could make you laugh at any time of the day or night. He was always laughing and always smiling. He was a little bit of a trickster too. Every time I see Rickey, I just start laughing.

Rickey was a very versatile player. He played at Jackson State with Walter Payton, and in fact, Rickey is Walter's uncle. Rickey was a good blocker, a great receiver, and a slippery kind of runner who could really get the ball down the field. He had good sense and instincts for the game. Bud liked him because he had the traits Bud was looking for: reliability, durability, and dependability. You could always rely on him to come through. If you needed two yards he would get four. That was Rickey.

Rick Danmeier was our kicker after Fred Cox retired. He was with us for about six years. A quiet player, he kept to himself most of the time. He may have been one of the last kickers to kick the ball straight on. I believe Mark Moseley of Washington was the last one. He was a good worker on the field and off. He was reliable; he did a tough job and did it well. Either you loved him or you didn't, depending on whether he made the kick. And Rick made most of them.

I can recall when Blair Walsh was with us. I was in the scouting department at the time and had not scouted him in college. He had phenomenal leg strength and had a great early part of his career. His first year was unbelievable. I will never forget when he missed that kick against Seattle in the 2015 NFC playoffs. I mean, it was unbelievable! It was a 27-yard chip shot at the end of the game. He missed it, the game was over, and the Vikings' season ended at that moment. And it did him in. He was never the same after that miss.

I had a dream the night before the game that Blair was going to kick the winning field goal, and I told Rob Brzezinski that before the kick. Well, I was wrong. Blair was a really good kid who went about his

business, which was always kicking. And when he wasn't, he was training in the weight room. I personally feel that he may have overtrained.
Ultimately I don't know what it was, but he was never the same. And
now he's out of the NFL completely.

Joey Browner played with me for a long time. He was an unbelievable talent. He had linebacker size and defensive back speed. He
was very physical and had extremely strong hands. He was about 225
pounds and six foot two. He could cover receivers, tight ends, and
running backs. He would play in the box (between the ends) because
he had such great ability. And he could physically line up on the edge
and do his job. Joey had tremendous skills as a player—Hall of Fame
credentials. He is a Ring of Honor player for the Vikings and I believe
he's one of those guys who could play today.

We only played together for one year, but it was clear that Cris
Carter was an exceptional player. He got things figured out early on in
his career and cleaned up his act. He had unbelievable ball skills. He
was quicker than he was fast and could really go and get the football.
He had unbelievable body control and super concentration. He was
a tremendous route runner who could get early separation from the
defensive backs. Good route runners like Cris have great attention to
detail. They started off the same foot. They cut off of the same foot.
They had the body control to find a way to get open. Cris had it all.
He was so reliable as a player, and if you needed five he would get you
ten. He is a great Hall of Famer who really understood the game and
the business—and he has a great story to tell. He is a good guy and a
good friend, and I respect him a lot.

Wade Wilson was a good friend and probably one of the nicest
guys I have ever known as a teammate. He went to a small Texas

school and needed to work hard on his mechanics when he got here—and he did. He worked his tail off every day and became a good, solid quarterback for us. He worked on his release and did drill after drill to get better. He led by example by going out there every day and doing his job. He was really good in the locker room; I know that everyone respected him. He died of a heart attack in his sleep on his 60th birthday. I miss him. He was a real friend who left us far too soon.

Ted Brown was a short, compact runner who was a really good guy. He was bigger than he looked. He had good balance, good feet, and could really carry the football. He also caught the ball well. He was our No. 1 back for a while and did a good job. Teddy was a good person and a very likable guy.

Darrin Nelson was unfortunately one of the five players who were part of the Herschel Walker trade with the Dallas Cowboys. Darrin was an outstanding player. He had good speed and had a good all-around game. He had good cuts and good ball skills. I was sorry to see him go.

One of the steadiest and most consistent players for us was Henry Thomas—a very underrated football player. He was as smart a player and as instinctive a player as you could ever find. As a lineman, Henry was never going to get the accolades others did. He was a little bit undersized during his time but he had unbelievable hands and great eyes. He really had a great overall feel for the game. He was the unsung hero of our front four and was the glue up front.

We were always on the same page mentally, and there is no question that Henry kept me in the league longer than I should have been. He had a great feel for blocking patterns and was a very disciplined football player. He rarely made a mistake and was always there doing the dirty work and what had to be done. He was just the steady Eddie of our group at the time. He is a great guy, a good family man, and a consummate professional. I don't think you could ever find a person who would say anything bad about Henry Thomas.

Most fans remember where they were when something big happened. And that was the way it was when the Vikings announced that they had made the trade with Dallas for Herschel Walker during the 1989 season. I first heard about the trade shortly after it was made. We were in team meetings and a few players were called out. Those were the players that we had traded to Dallas: Darrin Nelson, Jesse Solomon, David Howard, Isiaac Holt, and Alex Stuart.

Mike Lynn, the Vikings general manager, orchestrated the whole trade deal, and I think he did it behind closed doors. I'm not sure any of the coaching staff or scouting department knew anything about it. Mike felt the Vikings were in good shape to go to the Super Bowl but were missing one thing: the big back. And in Mike's mind, Walker was that back.

Also unbeknownst to anyone else, I think Jerry Jones and Jimmy Johnson just wanted the picks. They obviously didn't care anything about the players because they cut them all. I guess the deal was if the Cowboys cut any of the players then they got some of the picks. So when it was all over, the Cowboys got the Vikings' first pick for three years, the second pick for three years, the third pick for one year, and a sixth-round pick. I think it was all Mike Lynn's deal from beginning to end. He got so wrapped up in the trade that I'm not sure Mike even knew that the Cowboys were going to cut all of the players the Vikings sent.

Herschel was a big, fast, strong player who was a straight-ahead runner. His skills were very attractive to Mike. He was also a really good guy. He was a quiet, unassuming person who was very respectful to everyone. He wanted to do well. The game was very important to him. I thought he handled the whole situation very well. He came in here and went to work and did what he could to ingratiate himself to the team. I did a television thing with him on *Rosen's Sports Sunday* for quite a while. He was easy to work with and just an all-around nice person. Unfortunately, he never materialized as the back that Mike Lynn wanted. Herschel came into a very difficult situation and handled it pretty well. The expectations were so high he never could have lived up to them. He never set the world on fire, but he was a decent back for us. I guess I understand why Mike did it as the final piece to the puzzle, but it just didn't work out; worse, it sent the Vikings into somewhat of a tailspin for a few years after all the draft picks that we lost.

Fred Zamberletti is an icon in the organization—though I didn't see it that way in the beginning. The only interaction I ever had with Fred was when I got hurt. Unless you had an issue like that, you didn't have anything to do with Fred. As I got older, and especially after I retired, I came to see Fred as a great man. He was Bud's guy, and Bud depended on Fred a lot of the time. He was a well-rounded guy (he also loved the stock market) who gave his life to the Minnesota Vikings. He cared deeply and he had a lot of tough love for the players.

Dennis Ryan, the Vikings equipment manager, is the absolute best. He is very unassuming and one of the best people that I have ever known. He is always in the building. If you ask something from him, you will have it in the next few minutes. If any person has a bad thing to say about Dennis Ryan, then it is all on them, because Dennis is the nicest guy you would ever want to meet. He has been with the Vikings forever, and they will probably have to carry him out of the place. He is the most loyal individual you could ever find. Stubby Eason, the original equipment manager, hired Dennis himself, and he is the most hardworking, blue-collar guy. He has been a fixture at the place forever.

Paul Wiggin has been with the Vikings for a long time as well. He is a pretty special guy who is very intelligent. He played in the league for many years, coached in the league for a long time, and has been in personnel for us as well. Paul is very approachable, and you can talk to him about anything. He is very respectful and cares deeply about people. He works on the pro side of the team's scouting. He does breakdowns of the other teams for the coaching staff and also breaks down the defensive linemen of the other teams in addition to evaluating the defensive linemen for each draft class. He is a really classy guy and everyone thinks so highly of him. I have nothing but good things to say about Paul.

To any of those players or personnel that I missed in these pages, I want to say that I'm sorry. You have all meant a lot to me and I will never forget you. Thank you!

CHAPTER FIVE

Bud to Steckel
to Bud to Burns

Bud. The name stands out. All you have do to is mention his first name, and everyone will know who you are talking about. He was a man of very few words, and he had the most common-sense approach to the game of anyone I have ever known. But it was only after I retired that Bud opened up somewhat to me. I learned so much more about Bud in later years than I ever did while he was my coach.

I think he understood and realized a long time ago that he was going to be a really good coach if he had really good players. Bud knew that and he understood it very well. He demanded a very high level of respect just from the way that he carried himself. I believe he still would be a good coach today, but it might be harder for him now. With the money, free agency, other things, he would have to adapt some—and I know he would.

He always preached to us about reliability, dependability, and durability. That was who he was. I knew, and we knew, that in order to ingratiate yourself to Bud, he had to be able to rely on you on Sunday. He had to know each and every week that you were going to be ready to play football. He never communicated much with the defensive players—or the offensive players, for that matter—he let the assistant coaches do their thing.

When I came in as a first-year player, the team had been together for a long time and had just come off a Super Bowl season. Jim Marshall was the unquestioned leader of the team. Jeff Siemon and Matt Blair were the other leaders on the defense. It was a veteran-laden team that knew how to perform to Bud's directive. I was the newcomer and had to find my place.

Bud didn't have to raise his voice, yell, or scream. All he had to do was look at you and you knew. You just knew. There was a certain fear factor with Bud. You just knew that if you screwed up continually, you were going to be gone and that would be it. He was very intolerant of that kind of thing because it went against everything that he stood for. There was no one who coached me in my entire career who was like Bud. He was one in a million.

I had not expected Bud to leave when he did. In 1984 we were a middle-of-the-road football team; nothing monumental was supposed to happen. I don't know why things had changed for us. I mean, we operated downstairs and the management team operated upstairs, so to speak. It was in Mike Lynn's heyday. Sure, we probably had some misses in the draft, some injuries, and we struggled somewhat. But I had never given a thought to Bud leaving. It came as a complete surprise to me and most of the team.

I expected that Jerry Burns was going to be the head coach; I never expected Les Steckel to come in. I don't know what happened behind the scenes at all. I have my thoughts about it, but no facts to back any of it up.

Les had been with us for a while. He was the special teams coordinator, so I had a lot of interaction with him. I had a good relationship with him. But when he came in as our head football coach he didn't let things stand at all. He made wholesale changes throughout the organization and to the way the team operated. He was into everything we did. He brought in new coaches and planned to go his own way. I guess you are never ready for a change, but this one was dramatic. We really didn't know what to expect.

We had moved our base to Winter Park. We had some structure during the off-season to train and work out, but we had no idea as to what was coming. It turned out to be a living nightmare. Les had a military background, and he delivered it to us in full force. He structured it that way. We ran and we ran and we ran—and then when we thought we were all done running, we ran some more. It was brutal. It was like nothing any of us had ever seen before. Dennis Swilley, our starting center, ran his last of many 100-yard dashes, ran off the field into the locker room, took off his equipment, and never came back.

Les's training camp was horrific in every way. We had to climb ropes, run uphill and downhill. It was absolutely mind-boggling what he had us doing. Even if you were in good shape it was hard. If you were out of shape, it was absolutely unbelievable. But you had to do it. Everything was so different than what we had with Bud. With Bud you knew what he wanted and needed, and with Les it was 100 percent the opposite.

We had an ironman contest to start training camp that took place in the stadium in front of all of our fans. We had one guy, a fairly high draft choice, who fell while rope climbing, broke his ankle, and was out for the year. Those kinds of things happened, but to this day I have always wondered what the fans must have thought.

We were full contact, full pads almost every single day of training camp. We were competitive for the first four or five weeks of the regular season and then it caught up to us. Guys just quit on the team. We had a senior advisory committee that would meet with Les and give advice; none of it was acted upon. It just fell by the wayside.

I liked Les, but I don't think he was ready to be a head coach in the NFL. I don't think he had the experience to be a head coach and he didn't know what his style was going to be. That was so difficult for us players to cope with. He never started easy; he just went at it full force from the beginning.

When we started, we were still the same team that Bud had carried through the 1983 season. The latter half of the only season with Les, we were basically a M*A*S*H unit. We were so beaten up, it was pitiful. There was a lot of grumbling. The core of our football team did understand that we had a job to do, and despite everything that was going on, we had to go out and play on Sunday. We just were not good enough to go through all of it. The last part of the season was a real struggle because we were so beaten up and didn't have the players to compete.

It was a combination of a new head coach, average talent, and a lack of resiliency for the team to follow him, and it was a perfect storm for failure. We basically kind of fell apart. By the end of the year there were a lot of different cliques that had formed and it was hard to keep the locker room together. When we walked out on the field, though, I would say we remained professional. The game was still important to all of us.

I played the entire year and tried my best to play as hard as I could, but my intensity just wasn't there. I felt sorry for the players, the coaches, and even Les. He was a brand-new head coach and practically everything he did burst into flames. If he would have stayed, I'd like to believe that he would have changed a few things, but we will never know.

The last two games of the season were an absolute disaster. I mean, we were throttled. We were glad when it was finally over. To even play any more games would have been difficult. For the most part, the entire season was a complete bust. The day after the season ended we had a meeting downstairs at Winter Park. Mike Lynn came in and addressed the team. He told us that he had made the decision to let Les go and that he hoped that he would never have to do anything like that again. We could see that it was a very painful decision for Mike, but many of us were relieved.

It was very unusual for Mike to address the team like that. He was never around the players; he didn't come down to the field before or after games. I felt bad for the players, coaches, and for Les. But I think there was a collective sigh in the locker room. There was tremendous trauma suffered by everyone because of the way the season had gone, so there was no doubt that it caused some relief.

I don't think a lot of people realize the tremendous difficulty that a firing causes. It's sort of like getting cut from a team. It's over, and your entire family is affected by it. I was lucky that it never happened to me. I have seen it happen many times as a player. Outside of the game I have seen it happen too many times. There are often good reasons for letting someone go, but it is never easy. When I was the director of college scouting, I had to do it a couple of times. It was never personal for me, but it was something I had to do—and I never liked any aspect of it. Because of the salary cap, I know that we are going to go through some tough times when it comes to our roster today. People will have to be let go, and that's tough. It's tough on the team, it is tough on the guy having to do it, and it is really tough on the player.

When we heard that Bud was coming back, it was a tremendous relief. We knew Bud, knew what he expected, and we got the continuity back that we had once had. There was no repeat of anything that Les did when Bud returned. It was back to business as usual in 1985—and then Bud retired again.

I have to admit that I was a little surprised that Bud only stayed for a year, but he got things back on track. As a player, I was very glad to have Bud come back. He brought normalcy back to the organization. I can only assume there was some kind of an agreement that if Bud came back, when he left Jerry Burns would get the head coaching job. And that is exactly what happened. Bud had his style and way of doing things and then when he left for the second time, the coaching job went to Burnsie. He had his way of doing things too, but it was a lot closer to Bud's than it was to Steckel's.

I know it hurt Jerry a lot when he didn't get the job when Bud left the first time, and fortunately for us Jerry stayed. When Jerry got the job the transition was very smooth. He had been with us for a long time and he was a good guy, an excellent football coach, and we all knew he was going to keep things on track. And he did.

Every player in the locker room would have run through the wall for Burnsie. He was as beloved a coach as you could have. He knew football and he knew players, and it was just a great mix. Everyone was excited about the first season—and the rest of them as well—while he

A skinny high school football player on my 1970 team.

Lifting weights at the old training camp in Mankato. (Courtesy of the Minnesota Vikings)

Fielding an interception against Seattle. (Courtesy of the Minnesota Vikings)

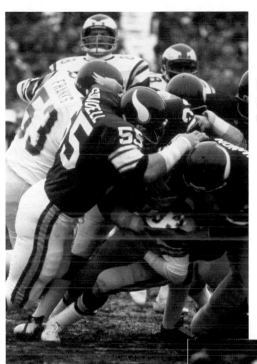

Putting a hurt on Philly in 1985. (Courtesy of the Minnesota Vikings)

Getting to Tampa Bay's quarterback Steve DeBerg. (Courtesy of the Minnesota Vikings)

Taking in the sights with pals Tommy Kramer and Matt Blair on an exhibition trip to London. (Courtesy of the Minnesota Vikings)

I played the game the only way I knew how: with intensity, passion, and enjoyment. (Courtesy of the Minnesota Vikings)

Being interviewed by former teammate Ahmad Rashad, along with teammate Wade Wilson. (Courtesy of the Minnesota Vikings)

Herschel and me on *Rosen's Sports Sunday.* (Courtesy of the Minnesota Vikings)

Banged up and bloodied, but always ready for action. (Courtesy of the Minnesota Vikings)

Community service was one of the most rewarding parts of the job. Here, Keith Millard and I visit pediatric patients and their families. (Courtesy of the Minnesota Vikings)

I also love giving autographs, especially to young fans. (Courtesy of the Minnesota Vikings)

It was a privilege to don the Purple and Gold for 14 seasons. (Courtesy of the Minnesota Vikings)

was in charge. Like him or love him, he was one of the great characters of the game. He was fun to play for—and I mean *really* fun. Every time he addressed the team, there was a lot of profanity, but everyone loved him. He was funny, and yet when he got serious we knew it was time to go to work. He was very approachable; guys liked to play for him. We understood what he wanted and, frankly, he wasn't a complicated guy. He was quite easy to figure out. We had some very good teams while Jerry was coach.

Jerry left after the 1991 season. I retired after my 14th season, the year before. I was 36 years old and I just couldn't do some of the things physically that I did the previous season. That last year they began to replace me on defense with a young player, Ray Berry. That was really tough. But once your physical skills start to leave you, you know it is time to go.

I knew during the season that this would be my last year. I played my entire career for the Minnesota Vikings. As the season went on, it became more and more evident that the time was coming for me. It was hard to swallow, but the handwriting was on the wall.

I had some conversations with Roger Headrick about potentially staying on after my playing days were over. He was one of the eight that ran the Vikings. I could not play at a level where I was satisfied. It wasn't working for me any longer, and I had no idea what I was going to do after retirement. I didn't have any concrete plans. I knew we were going to stay in town because my wife is from here. But what I was going to do for the rest of my life was totally unknown.

Finally about four months into my retirement, my wife came to me and asked, "What do you want to do now that football is over for you?" I knew it was time to find something. I knew that I wanted to stay in football but I did not want to coach. Coaching and working with the players every day would have been great, and I know that I would have loved it, but it is too uncertain. Changing jobs and moving every few years was not for me or for my family.

I was lucky that Roger Headrick created a position for me. I was kind of a liaison to the players for management. I took over that responsibility in the beginning, as his assistant—assistant to the president. I was kind of split between two different jobs. I was doing the league stuff for Roger and then I was doing the football stuff—quality control like breaking down film for the football side of it. The liaison stuff was tough on me because I was so close to the team and the players, so I gravitated more toward the football side of it. Within about a year, I began scouting and I settled in. Little did I know that it was the beginning of another long career: in scouting for the Minnesota Vikings.

CHAPTER SIX

The End Had Come

The Vikings were now being run by not one but eight owners. Roger Headrick was the main man, in the president's role. And I was a new-comer to the other side of the organization. Football had been my whole life as a player. I played for 14 years and loved every minute of it.

It was a complete joy every day to go to work, and I relished every aspect of it. I am so fortunate that I was able to stay healthy and play as long as I did. I know that through the years I met a lot of people who impacted my life, and I hope I was able to do the same for others.

If you have a job that you love, you will never work another day in your life. There are a lot of people in this world who do not like their jobs. They hate to go to work, many more than you would ever know. I know that I was not one of them, and that's why I consider myself so lucky. I was extremely blessed to get drafted in the ninth round by the Minnesota Vikings. I found a way to stick with the club, and the rest is history.

When Les was here it was difficult in many ways, but there was a silver lining to it: I still enjoyed coming to work. I still enjoyed playing on Sundays. I still relished my teammates. But it was a difficult year. Number one, because of the way we finished and the way we all felt about it—we only won three games. It was a tough year psychologically for everybody. Maybe when you look back it helped people grow. We survived it and moved on.

I think looking forward to going to work every day was the norm for most of the National Football League players then. Some players played for different reasons—maybe the wrong reasons—but for the most part I think most players understand that they have a certain skill set that most people don't have. They have had the opportunity to play a game at the highest level and get compensated for it. The competition is the very best; you won't find any better competitors in the entire world. I think that the players back then, and today, really relish that challenge.

Salaries today are unbelievable, but it is all relative. When I came into the league it was still kind of a mom-and-pop shop. Players were not making a ton of money. Maybe the top players were making $100,000 or a little more. I was happy with my $22,000 a year.

Football today is a billion-dollar business. Tremendous television money goes to each team along with a lot of other resources. That's just the way it is.

The guys who came before me in the league made less money than I did, and the guys who came after me make a lot more. For me, it was never about the money; it was always about the experience and the profession. I'm happy for the players today. The way I look at it, as long as they earn it, I'm all for it.

I played from 1977 to 1990. Back then it was still a very run-oriented game, and throwing the ball was more of a necessity than the norm. I sometimes wonder if I could have played the game as it is today. The style of the defense and most everything about the game is so different—but then I have to slap myself and say, "Of course I could! I would just have to adjust."

The old run-oriented style certainly fit my game more. I think I came along at just the right time. I got drafted by a team that needed a backup linebacker on their roster, so the timing was perfect. I made it, and lasted a long time. I was disappointed that I didn't get drafted until the ninth round, but as I look back, it was the right time for me. And it worked out.

I'm sure I could not have played any longer. My last year, I stretched it as long as I could. I got hurt. I broke my ribs and was hurt for some time. Ray Berry was coming on then as our middle linebacker. I would start the games, but then after a few plays I would come out and Ray would come in. I had become more of a spot player and a special teams player. I couldn't do what I used to be able to do.

By the end, it was much harder for me physically. It was harder emotionally as well. I knew I was getting phased out. I probably could have hung on for one more season, but I knew the end had come for me. I knew when I started to lose interest in some of the things that previously I had been excited about, the handwriting was on the wall. I had to be honest with myself, the organization, my teammates, and my family. It was time.

It wasn't always my goal to stay in football after I retired. I wasn't exactly sure what I was going to do or in fact wanted to do. Roger Headrick and I had some conversations during my last season about various things I might like to do in the organization. We talked about it a few times in passing or on airplanes, but nothing really stuck with me. Until my wife, Jenny, made that comment—"What the hell are you going to do?"—frankly, I hadn't given it a whole lot of thought.

About five months after my final season ended, an opportunity came up. Roger apparently had seen something in me that he wanted to explore, so we kind of kicked things around for a while. I started my second career on June 1, 1991, when I signed on with the Vikings as assistant to the president. It was a big change. It was not a job that was really defined to start; my role was certainly a work in progress.

John Wooten, who had played in the league for a long time and was an advocate for the players, started a program in the league office to help players get involved in the community, finish their degrees, work jobs in the off-season, and improve upon a wide variety of life skills. Today we have a full-time staff that does so much for the players with every issue that you could imagine.

I was still too close to the players to make this role work very well. I had a hard time separating work from friendships. At the same time that year, I was doing some work with the defensive staff. Although I was not a coach, I did some quality-control work for the Vikings, and I really enjoyed that aspect. It was the only football-related part of my job at that time.

I loved the football aspect and I could have gone into coaching except for one thing. Job security was definitely an issue. The turnover rate was very high. I didn't want that for my family. My wife is from Minnesota, we had small kids at the time, and I didn't want to move. I loved helping the coaching staff, but I wasn't on the coaching staff, just helping out. Sure, it would have been unbelievable to have played here and coached here, but it was not in the cards.

As a player, I was always very comfortable in my role here all those years. I never worried about being traded or cut from the team, but I always geared myself up with the belief that every year I was going to have to make this football team. I think you have to be honest in your evaluations of yourself. I never got threatened by the coaching staff that I might be traded or anything like that. It was more of a personal goal of mine to prove to myself I earned it.

With Bud, I never needed any pats on the back, any "attaboys." Bud was very quiet. He could just look at you the wrong way and you knew. That was all it took—you had fallen out of favor, had done something wrong, or were not playing by the rules. You always knew.

I was very familiar with Bud's style and I never got that look from Bud. I think he realized that once I got between the lines, it was very important to me. Again, he was always a stickler for reliability, durability, and dependability. I felt I fit those criteria, and never really felt threatened by him at all. I always believed he knew how much the game meant to me, and I tried to show him on Sundays.

When Jerry Burns came in I was probably more comfortable with him than with Bud because there was more conversation with Burnsie. Bud always kept his emotions in check and held everything pretty close to the vest. He was a very private person, and that spilled over into his public life as well. By contrast, Jerry Burns was an open book. I'm not saying there was anything wrong with Bud's style, but players felt like Jerry was more approachable and opened up more to the players. Theirs were two different styles, and they worked well for each of them.

Everyone was a little afraid of Bud. It was not because he was mean or anything like that, but his style made the players somewhat uncomfortable. But it was simple: if you just went out and did your job every day, there was no issue or any problem at all.

When Jerry left after the 1991 season, I can say for sure that it had nothing to do with my decision to end my playing career. I just knew after 14 years my time as a player had come to an end.

When Roger set it up for me to work for him as the assistant to the president, it was great. He was a very cordial individual and I enjoyed working for him. When he came in he took over Mike Lynn's office, and although he wasn't doing the contracts, he did fulfill many of the duties that Mike had. The contracts at the time were handled by Jeff Diamond and a few others.

He was the managing business partner of the eight owners. I don't exactly know how they came to the decision as to who was going to actually run the club, but Roger was the one. He was intelligent and understood that he was not a football guy. He had been very successful as a businessman but never pretended to know football like the football people did. He was a good listener. I think he enjoyed spending time around the football people, and I think he learned a lot from the coaches, scouts, and those connected to the game. Some of the professional minds we had at the time were brilliant, and Roger liked being around them. He was like a sponge, sucking it all in.

At some point they asked me if I would be interested in the scouting side of things. I had no idea how complicated this side of the business was. When I first started hearing about all they did, it was mind-boggling to say the least.

In the beginning it sounded interesting, so I dabbled in it a little bit. I found out the number of days the Vikings scouts were on the road doing scouting. Conrad Cordano took me out for the first time in the spring of 1992—he was our West Coast and BLESTO scout at the time. Conrad taught me a lot and became a wonderful friend.

At the time and still today there are two types of scouts, with some crossover: college scouts and the pro scouts. They cross paths during the draft meetings, but for the most part the college scouts stay out of the way of the pro personnel. The Vikings had several veteran scouts there when I started. There was Conrad, Ralph Kohl, Johnny Carson, and Don Deisch. Murray Warmath came in a little later.

When I made the transition to scouting after the first year, it was a blessing for me. I had been in the office every day and was around the scouts, and we got along very well. The scouting staff was a very veteran staff that had been together for a long time. My bosses were Jerry Reichow and Frank Gilliam. Jerry was the head of the department and had been a Vikings player. He played in the first-ever Vikings game in 1961 and had been a solid receiver for the team. Frank was the one who ran the draft of college players and set the board. He really knew the business. Back then it was all handwritten labels and typed-up lists. There were no computers or cell phones, much less the modern technology that we use today.

I became a college scout working mostly in the Midwest. Once I started full-time on the scouting side, it felt like a perfect fit. Down the road, once Jerry Reichow took on a more limited role and moved out of state, I absorbed most of his in-house work and got much more involved. But when I first started in the scouting department, I can honestly say I knew absolutely nothing about scouting. I mean, I didn't know who did what, who looked for what, or anything. I have to laugh when I think about it because it was about as foreign to me as if I'd started a new career completely out of football.

I started getting a feel for things. I had to learn about going to schools and how to handle myself with the coaches and others. I had to learn who the people were—who I could trust and who I couldn't. Some of them were very open and honest and some not so much. Ultimately I learned that experience was the best teacher.

I learned how to work an area and how to decipher the information and navigate the workload. At first it was all handwritten reports. We would write them, make copies, and send them in. From there they would be put in books and locked into a large safe at the Vikings offices. Kelly Wilske, who was our administrative assistant for more 30 years, did a fabulous job keeping us organized.

There were so many players we looked at during a given season. I worked hard at it and tried not to get frustrated. If I spent a lot of time with one player and another team ended up drafting him, it didn't bother me. There was always someone else we would draft, or we'd take a shot on as a free agent.

All the scouts were accountable to every school and every prospect in our respective areas, so the pool was always very large. I knew that my opinion counted just as much as the other veteran scouts', but you might go into a draft with reports totaling into the hundreds, and not one of those players would get drafted by us. That's just the way it was.

Frank Gilliam ran the draft. Bud's staff was not heavily involved in the draft, while Jerry Burns's staff was a little more involved. Denny Green came to the coaching ranks after Jerry Burns, and his staff was more intricately involved.

As the years went by, the coaches got much more involved. The staff I worked with was very respectful of each person's individual role. We always had a staff that understood how the system worked. Frank and Jerry did a great job with the draft and managing the process.

I happen to know that there are teams that don't even allow the scouting staff into the room during the draft, but the Vikings have never been that way. The scouts work their tails off for 10 months out of the year and have a very personal investment in their work, so to be included is very important to them. They deserve to be in there and appreciate it; the draft is their game day.

When Mike Lynn ran the Vikings he would get involved indirectly. Unfortunately, he engineered the very infamous Herschel Walker trade with Dallas that set the Vikings back for a few years. Roger did not get involved much at all. Instead, he just would sit in the room to listen to the banter. I think he enjoyed being around the personnel people— but he understood his boundaries. He was respectful of our individual roles just as we would not sit in and contribute to ownership agendas. Everybody stayed in their lanes. I do think Roger did like the football side of it, but knew how to let it go to the people who did the work. He learned a lot from those meetings, but it was not his job to oversee it, so he left it alone. He knew where he belonged and was extremely professional.

There were seven other owners in addition to Roger, but they all left the football business to the football people. They would be around at times, especially Wheelock Whitney, but they never interfered much on a daily basis. For the most part they remained on the sideline. I'm sure they had their opinions, but we never heard them—just like we didn't share what we did. We knew when they were there, but they didn't get in our business. They were owners, period.

When I started in the scouting department. I was called the college scouting coordinator. I moved up in the ranks until I became the scouting director, a title I held for a number of years.

I have been asked one question many times that is somewhat of a difficult one to answer. The question was, "How does a scout miss on a player? Guys like John Randle, Mick Tingelhoff, and others—guys who are never drafted but play their way into the Pro Football Hall of Fame. How does that happen?"

Every team has their own different style, their own format, and then every scout is a little bit different. You can tell the scouts who are big measurable scouts—all about height, weight, and speed. Does the player fit into those parameters?

I was a huge production grader. Those who made plays in college got the high marks from me. I felt that typically they would find a way to make plays at our level. But when you get to the NFL the players are all bigger, stronger, and faster—a definite difference from college football. The competition is much greater, so you have to figure out if this guy has the ability to take his particular skill set to the next level.

There will always be guys who will fall through the cracks and you'll miss them, but you need to get a lot of them right too. There are not as many who fall through the cracks now because everything is so comprehensive. Our guys evaluate more than a thousand players over the course of the fall and spring. Some you find or already know are just a little too slow or just a little too small but you still take a look at them.

John Randle came in here at 245 pounds. One of our scouts, Don Deisch, loved the way Randle played. His fire and competitive nature were outstanding. He just battled and fought and clawed. He continued to get bigger and better and better, and the bottom line was that we rolled the dice based on Don's conviction and signed Randle to the Vikings...and he made it all the way to the Pro Football Hall of Fame. I mean, this guy came in as a free agent and made it to the Hall. John was an unbelievable player who was just plain and simply missed in the draft. Fortunately, we picked him up as a free agent.

It was the same with Mick Tingelhoff. There are a lot of guys who fall through the cracks and end up making it because of their great instincts and their competitive spirit. These guys have an unbelievable work ethic and they've got heart. On the flip side, there are guys that have all the measurable characteristics—everything on paper says they are going to make it. But they don't have the passion and the heart for the game, so they fail. They lack the drive and everything that goes with it. Those are the ones that haunt you, drive you nuts. If you examine the first rounds every year, there are always players that don't make it.

I evaluate players by how big and fast they are and whether they can do the things expected of them. But I also try my best to measure their heart, drive, attention to detail, passion, and instincts. Of course, trying to measure passion is very difficult. After you get through the basics, I looked for the right instincts. Do I see an agile player? Do I see a competitive player? Do I see a player that plays with high emotion and passion? Does he make plays? If you watch long enough you can tell—well, most of the time anyway.

There are so many variables to consider for each individual position. A great deal of it is about what the player does on game day. There were parameters that we used for every position. The players, especially today, are dissected from every angle.

When we look at the data for a player, the real difficulty is determining whether he can take all that to the next level. Can he make it? Will he make it? Or will he fall by the wayside? We really don't know. A "sure thing" may in fact fail. All you can do is learn about a player and hope for the best. It was a tough job, but I loved doing it.

CHAPTER SEVEN

Scouting

My move to scouting was a natural transition. In the beginning of my scouting career, I was heavily involved in administrative things, such as getting ready for the draft. Everything was done by hand. My job was to check the waiver list every day and to keep our pro board for all the other NFL teams up to date. That was a big job in itself. It was essentially maintaining the rosters of every team in the league. That meant checking the waivers, monitoring any trades that were made, and anything else personnel-related that might need to be known.

Frank Gilliam and Jerry Reichow pretty much let me do my thing and left me alone. They gave me some guidelines to follow, but I learned on the job. Today everything is done electronically, but back then it was a visual board that everyone used. There was no automation at all.

Evaluating the players and getting the correct information was the key to everything. Most teams use the type of player its head coach wants on the team as their evaluation crutch. I would look for what

I knew was important to the head coach and his staff—and I worked for many, so my evaluations varied depending on who was in charge.

In the spring of my first year in scouting, I went out on the road with Conrad Cardano. I went to some of the schools where players were being tested with measurable results—Wyoming, UNLV, and some other schools out west. Conrad was a BLESTO scout. BLESTO stands for Bears, Lions, Eagles, Saints Talent Organization. The Vikings organization had scouts that worked for their BLESTO team, and the information that they put together was shared among the BLESTO teams. I learned a lot from Conrad, and he was a great mentor.

The BLESTO scouts would generate a list of all of the college seniors who they felt would be good candidates. The players would then be evaluated on tape and that tape shared with all of the involved clubs. When we went into schools we would look at players who were recommended to us by BLESTO. And there were always additional players who would pop up at the schools.

The country was sectioned off by region. Conrad was responsible for all the schools in his area, including Montana, Wyoming, Utah, Colorado and the other western schools. When I first became an area scout, I covered North Dakota, South Dakota, Kansas, Nebraska, Missouri, Arkansas, Minnesota, Wisconsin, Michigan, Ohio, Indiana, and Illinois. I might visit as many as 45 to 50 schools in the fall. And once I became the director of college scouting for the Vikings, I was basically responsible for the entire country. I would see as many players as I could before the draft, generating hundreds of player reports.

When we went out to a school, we generally knew who we were going to be looking at ahead of time. Being a member of the BLESTO scouting organization we would get information covering the majority of the schools in the country, at every division level. There was a certain area of the country that each of the BLESTO scouts would work, and we would get the information from them late in the spring after the draft, which would allow us to put together our schedules for the fall. We had to apportion time for the school visits, film evaluation, and of course, looking at the players. There were hundreds of schools that we had to get to once July and August rolled around. The area, regional, and national scouts would all put their schedules together in preparation for the upcoming college season.

Looking at the players we always looked for what the head coaches and staff wanted, as well as other intangibles. Here is the way we would evaluate the various positions:

DEFENSIVE END

We had certain parameters we used for evaluation—height, weight, arm length, in addition to test scores. When Mike Zimmer came to the Vikings, we found out quickly that he wanted big, tall, long-armed guys who could bend and accelerate into contact. He liked the big guys, so you always had that in the back of your mind. When you looked at a player, say this player was only six foot one and a half, maybe only 255 pounds, or maybe he doesn't have the kind of length that Mike is looking for. He could still be an exceptional player taking into account different kinds of measurables, such as quickness and production.

You can't just cookie-cut players. As a scout you have to base your evaluation on how they play the game and how they look during the games. Even if they don't meet Mike's criteria, you know that more of our scouts are going to cross-check the player, and you may potentially have varied opinions. Still, Mike's criteria are on the front burner.

I played with a guy named Al Noga. He did not have the ideal height and weight, but he was a great natural football player. He played with great effort and was relentless to the ball—a good all-around player. There are a lot of guys who don't quite meet your set criteria but have other parts to their game that make them outstanding players. Some are situational players rather than starters, but you still know they are going to play a lot.

DEFENSIVE TACKLE

The nose tackle is going to be a bigger and stronger man. He is a guy who can occupy two people, someone who can hold the point. He has good push but maybe does not have the quickness or acceleration that your under tackle may have.

Our under tackle is a little more streamlined and can move a little better. But each, with his own abilities, can be a big player for your football team. Under tackles generally have get-off quickness and can collapse edges of the opposition. They generally have the ability to be better pass rushers if the position calls for it.

Your under tackle may be your every-down player, whereas the nose tackle may come out of the game at times. The Vikings have had some great players at these positions going way back to Alan Page, Johnny Randle, Kevin Williams, Keith Millard, Henry Thomas, Pat Williams, and so many others who played in that position.

Henry didn't have the prototypical size for a nose tackle but he was one of the smartest players I have ever been around. He played with unbelievable leverage and phenomenal instincts. He had a great feel for the game. He played much bigger than he was. He had a great career. He may never have passed the eyeball test, but all you had to do was turn on the film and see how the guy worked and how intelligent he was. Henry was a great player for us and worthy of mentioning twice.

LINEBACKER

The linebacker position has become more specialized today. We have a "Mike" backer in the middle and a "Sam" backer on the strong side. The "Will" backer is the third type and probably the best athlete of the three. He probably has the best range, the best cover skills, can run, could be a three-down player, and is just better skilled overall.

Eric Kendricks doesn't have the ideal size for Mike, but he is a phenomenal player. He has great cover skills, unbelievable instincts, a nose for the football. He is very productive and does everything so well. When I evaluated him I thought he might have some trouble playing the Mike position and holding up, but he has been able to stay healthy. He has been durable, dependable, and very smart. He is one of those guys who likely didn't pass the eyeball test but has proven himself to be one of the very best linebackers in all of professional football. He has started since his second or third game as a rookie. Eric is everything that you are looking for in a linebacker and is an every-down player.

When I scouted Anthony Barr he fell into the category where we have a term called "Pet Cat." A Pet Cat was typically one of a scout's favorite players, despite the opinions of other scouts who evaluated him. Anthony is also Mike Zimmer's Pet Cat. He played with his hand in the dirt as a defensive end at UCLA. We could see that he had all the physical traits to be a great linebacker. He was tall and long and could run like a deer. He was very athletic. I was a little hesitant because I didn't see Anthony play off the ball that much. I just didn't know how quickly he would pick up the pro game and learn what he had to do to be successful. No doubt he has the ability and the mentality. He's an extremely intelligent player as well. But it was a natural transition and he grew into the position quickly. It took him a while to get his feet wet as a linebacker in our scheme, but he definitely has all the tools to be a great linebacker for a long time in the NFL. Kendricks and Barr are almost polar opposites, but their abilities, attitudes, and play-making skills make them both great football players.

DEFENSIVE BACK

The defensive back position has evolved somewhat over time. Back when I was playing we had a strong safety and a free safety; now the positions are interchangeable. You want your bigger, more physical player closer to the line of scrimmage. The way we play our coverages today—a heavy man scheme, because that's the way Mike Zimmer coaches—we have to try to find the defensive backs that fit into those schemes.

Some guys are more effective if they are closer to the line of scrimmage and others do their best off the line. Joey Browner was a great defensive back for us and was at his best closer to the line. He had the size of a linebacker and the speed and agility of a defensive back. We liked to keep Joey closer to the ball, but he was very efficient at both.

We look for a little bit of each—the big player and the smaller, faster individual—but every system has different wants and needs, with some carryover. Mike Zimmer likes his safeties to be able to handle man-to-man coverage; it doesn't matter whether it is a running back or a slot receiver, he wants his guys to be able to cover them. Take Harrison Smith, for example. He is a better player close to the line of scrimmage, coming downhill and playing in the box—and he is better attacking the football.

When Zimmer was in Dallas he got spoiled with a great defensive back in Deion Sanders. I mean, Sanders could do *everything*. Today he has a great number of back-end players who can stay with a receiver all day long. The man-to-man scheme can be very effective when you have shutdown corners, but it can hurt you when you lose some of your regular players and have to go with rookies, guys who have the physical skills but lack the experience. Then some adjustments have to be made.

Mike has a great defensive mind, and there is no question about the type of player he wants. He wants players up in opponents' faces. He likes putting a lot of pressure on the opposing offense, getting after the quarterback. He wants corners who can run all day and safeties who can cover like corners and hit like linebackers. The 2020 season seemed to be more challenging because we lost a lot of veteran players and have a lot of younger players, so they had to play a lot more zone coverage. In the zone defense, you can hide your young player a little better than in man-to-man coverage, and the mistakes aren't so glaring.

When you are evaluating a player you do look at the player's ability first and foremost, but you then try to fit him into the parameters the head coach wants. There is a fine line between the two, but somehow it seems to work out. If the player has good feet, good hips, good awareness of his situation, good instincts for the position, then he should be able to transition into the team's scheme. Even if his college team was a heavy zone team, the player should still have the ability to adjust to man-to-man coverage. It might take him a little time, but generally it should be okay. Scouts look for the physical traits first, then the intangible traits and mental traits. They recognize that the defensive back's job is probably the toughest job in football, other than perhaps quarterback. When you get good ones, it certainly does make Sundays easier.

Players can be good for a while and then suddenly go downhill and there can be many reasons. If the defensive back is a big guy, his weight can be a problem. DBs have to watch their weight very carefully. A heavy corner can be very sluggish if he doesn't watch it closely.

Money can be a factor too. Some players feel that once they receive that big paycheck, they don't have to work as hard anymore. What you want to find is the guy who isn't playing for the money but rather the guy who is playing to get better and better as a football player. I felt I was that kind of guy. Sure, the money was important to me, but the game and my ability to play were above anything else. You have to be a great student of the game and find ways to constantly improve. Everybody plays for a lot of different reasons, but the guy who has the great passion for the game, keeps himself in shape, constantly works at it, studies, and spends extra time on his craft—that's the kind of guy who typically doesn't have contract issues and those kinds of things. I don't begrudge anyone wanting to make more money, but they have to earn it. When they don't, it is hard to justify paying them.

CENTER

The center is the starting point to every offensive play. They can be a little more undersized. You can maybe hide them to a certain extent based on your scheme, but they run the show up front, so they have to have the smarts and all the intangibles. You are looking for guys who have good first-step quickness. You are looking for guys who have good balance and intelligence because they are the ones making all the calls and adjustments up front on the line.

Look at Matt Birk. Matt was a tremendous player for us, and then for the Ravens for years. It's a bonus if you can get a guy who's six foot four and 310 pounds. A lot of times centers may struggle going up against some of those bigger defensive tackles, but if they have all of the intangibles they will likely do well. They have to have the quickness to gain the edge on the opponent. They will get help from time to time in blocking schemes but they are the de facto quarterback of the offensive line and run the show.

They have to have the ability to work up to blocking the linebackers or second level, so they need good mobility and good range. They also have to be able to snap and step with a 300-pounder on their nose, and have more quickness and great balance to be able to counter that size and strength. I do think Garrett Bradbury has all of the traits you're looking for in the position. He should be a fixture in Minnesota for years to come.

GUARD

Size is a big plus at the guard position. They can be anywhere up to six foot seven, but typically a guard should be around six foot five and 325 pounds. They also have to have a certain arm length. They have to be agile enough to transition in the "phone booth" and have quick enough foot and body control to stay frontal on opponents.

You would like your guards in particular to be able to play more than one position, such as center or even tackle. You want the guards to be more physical players because they block the big people inside.

They have to have good functional strength but also good enough feet to stay under control against the defensive linemen. They can work up to the second level of blocking.

They probably don't have to be as athletic as the center or the tackle, but they are the big bangers inside. Size, strength, toughness, balance, and recovery ability are all essential. That said, the better athletes are typically going to be your centers and tackles. The big, tough guys who can survive inside are your guards. Ed White was the premier guard for us years back. Eddie had all the attributes. But when he went to San Diego, I think he eventually played tackle for them.

OFFENSIVE TACKLE

You would like the tackle to have the weight, height, arm length, feet, and mobility. They can be as big as six foot eight and weigh as much as 330 pounds. They don't have to be as strong as the guards because they don't usually block the big interior linemen. They protect the quarterback most of the time, blocking the defensive ends. They have to have the speed, quickness, and athleticism to move around more.

Reilly Reiff, our left tackle, survived on his instincts, awareness, and toughness. He did a great job for us. Brian O'Neill has it all, and like Reilly can play either position. They have to have the footwork to stay square on contact and not give up the edge.

When you boil it all down, you may say that this guy is a better right tackle than he is a left tackle, but he should be able to play either position. Assuming the quarterback is right-handed, which most are, it's the left tackle who must have the better length, feet, quickness, agility, and mobility. They have to be able to protect the quarterback's blind side. They don't have to be road graders, but they have to be able to knock people off the ball and they have to be able to combination block with the guards. Overall, we look for our tackles to be good athletes with size, toughness, and grit.

As I said before, most teams want to meet the standards of the head coach at each position. And we go out and look for the players that our coaches are looking for. Vikings GM Rick Spielman basically sets the tone for our team's roster, with the assistance of Mike Zimmer and Rob Brzezinski, so we take all that into account. We are always grading players based on Rick's criteria in conjunction with Mike's. Luckily, Rick and Mike are on the same page and have a very good working relationship.

TIGHT END

Tight ends used to be more like small tackles when the game was more run-oriented. Today, if you can get a player who has the length, size, and speed, then you are on the right track. Can he collapse the edge as a blocker and can he release to be a good receiver as well as a blocker both in-line and in space? Ideally, you would like to have a number of all-around-type players at tight end, but that is not always the case. The guys who can stay on the field for three downs and create matchup issues are the guys you want.

Stu Voigt was an excellent player for us many years back. He had phenomenal ball skills and was a great blocker. He was better known for his blocking, but it was well-known that when you threw the ball to Stu, he was going to catch it. Steve Jordan was another great tight end for us. He turned into a good blocker and was an excellent all-around football player. He had the intelligence and was a tireless worker. He had some huge games for the Vikings, and he played at a high level for a long time. He is a Ring of Honor player who, as I said, should be in consideration for the Pro Football Hall of Fame.

QUARTERBACK

Of course your quarterback needs to have all the measurables: size, arm strength, intelligence, the ability to put up big numbers. Every team is always looking for that quarterback with the "it" factor. Can they forget the losses? Can they put the bad games to bed? Can they put the team on their back at crunch time and carry them to victory?

You are looking for a great leader—a guy with great poise, anticipation, mobility…all the things that make them stand out. Once they get to this level and perform over a long period of time, then you know you have one. It is the hardest job in football and the most difficult to evaluate. The role has changed so much over the years, but it's become the focal point of the football team. And when you find a good one, you will always have a chance; when you don't, you have to find other ways to win.

RUNNING BACK

There are a lot of fundamentals that you look at with the running backs when you are trying to evaluate them. The first things you look at are height, weight, speed, and test scores. Then you look for the intangibles. You look at his ability to learn football. You look at his skill set. Is he a scat back or a straight-line, downhill runner? Or is he a combination of the two? How does he catch the ball? How does he block? Can he pick up stunts and blitzes? What kind of ball skills does he have? What kind of contact balance does he have? Is he a multiple-cut runner or is he a one-cut back? Does he have the speed to outrun angles? What kind of blocker is he? Can he give the proper protection? What kind of numbers does this kid put up on a game-day basis? Is he a workhorse? Is he a third-down back or a situational runner? There are so many different things that you look at.

Running back is a tough job, because every time they carry the ball they are going to get hit. They have got to be tough. They have got to be durable. They have to have good feet and good hips. They have to be able to bounce outside to the perimeter and be willing and able to run inside. They have to be able to stand up in protection against both linebackers and defensive linemen.

We also want to know what kind of production they have and what their yards per carry is. Are they every-down players or are they two-down players? Are they mudders or are they sprinters? There are a lot of different variables that you get in the running back. It is very rare when you find one who can do it all. Adrian Peterson was one, and he was and still is a great NFL back.

I evaluated Dalvin Cook. He was everything that was advertised about him. He was a very explosive player at Florida State. He ran bigger than he is. He has great contact balance, very good vision, and had big-play potential. He could make a 35-yard run out of a 5-yard carry. He had a world of potential and has lived up to it.

At the collegiate level, he struggled a little with catching the ball, but mainly because they didn't throw to him that much. He has improved a lot in that area; he has really worked at it and has done a great job. He has exceeded every expectation that we had when we drafted him. When he is healthy, he is one of the best backs in the league.

You would like to always have a combination of runners in your stable, so to speak. We like to have a big back on the roster, as well as a back like Dalvin, and we have that big back in Alexander Mattison. There used to be a time when we would have a much smaller back, a third-down back, but a guy like that couldn't take the day-in-and-day-out pounding that the bigger back can take. Still, you like to have a variety of guys who can bring different skill sets to the table as receivers and runners. There are just a lot of different flavors of backs.

WIDE RECEIVERS

You are always looking for the Randy Moss–type receiver—the guy who can take over a game—but those don't come along very often. Wide receivers come in every different shape and size. They all have unique traits. Some are possession receivers, who are usually the bigger athletes. They're guys that can run through the zones and take the top off the coverage.

There are the inside receivers and the outside receivers and the slot receivers, and then there are guys who are interchangeable. They have to have ball skills and toughness to be able to take the shots that some of these guys take. They have to have mental toughness and physical toughness, as well as great concentration. The guys who are precise route runners like Adam Thielen know how to get open and can run through cracks without losing any acceleration.

Justin Jefferson has great hand speed. He can be running full speed and then right at the point of catching the ball, he brings his hands up, so as not to telegraph that the ball is coming. He has unique savvy, and is a great route runner with great quickness. He has the natural skill set and instincts to continue to grow. I believe he will be a rising star in the league for a long time. It's very hard for these young receivers to come in and produce right away because of the complexities of the pro game. Jefferson gets it, and it looks like he is going to be a fixture with the Vikings for a long time.

Our administrative assistant, Kelly Wilske, would generate the original contact and set the date for our school visits. Some of them had restrictions and some had none. I was always very respectful of what the schools wanted. There was typically a coach on the team who was assigned to be the liaison, and I would call him. It was always very important to me to do what the schools wanted. I never tried to overstep my bounds or do anything that I thought was against school protocol. You would tell them when you were coming in or would like to come in, and they would then set it up.

When I went out to the schools, the Vikings did not have a dress code, so I would dress casually: shorts and a golf shirt in the warm months and blue jeans and a shirt or sweater in the winter. You wore what you needed to wear to stay warm or cool.

Generally they would first set you up in a film room to start to evaluate the players. Then at some point they would come in and you would talk about the players. After that you would usually attend practice and head down the road to the next school.

I tried to get to know the contact person at each school, and it was very important to me to be well-liked and well respected. Those relationships would pay dividends in the long run. Most of the people I met at the schools were great people, and I looked forward to seeing them every year. And the better we got along, the easier my job became. I enjoyed it very much and looked forward to seeing those people every season.

I think of scouting as the research and development part of a football team. We were always in the business of looking for fresh young talent so it was a necessary process—and I enjoyed it very much. Of course, there were some aspects that I liked better than others. The time away from home was very difficult. I mean, I was essentially on the road 200-plus days a year, sometimes two weeks or more at a time. We were basically gone for about nine months out of the year, and even when I was home, it was hard to keep my mind off of the job. I tried, but it was tough to do. My work was very important to me, and a lot of times my family took a back seat to my job.

There are certain kinds of people in this world. There is one kind that puts in just enough time to get the job done but never has a personal investment in the work. For those people it is just a job—no more, no less. For me, it was different. I lived the job, and it was very hard for me to turn it off. That's just the way I was.

When we went into schools and did our job, we created player reports. And there were *a lot* of them. I was a terrible typist and scared of technology, so for the most part I handwrote everything. Nowadays, reports are digital. Everything I did was done by hand and then I would generate just the final report by computer.

When I went to a school I might have to get information on as few as one player or as many as eight or nine. A premier place like Ohio State might have 10 or 11. Today, with all of the juniors that come out early for the draft, the workload has increased immensely. With juniors, you cannot be very aggressive as a scout; you more or less wait for someone to say something to you about it. It is a very touchy subject to say the least, but what can't be argued is that it sure does increase our workload.

For the most part you didn't visit with any players at the schools other than watching them practice. Some of the smaller schools might bring the kids around to visit, but for the most part you tried to be invisible when you were there.

I knew there were other scouts who at times did a little more than what was in the unwritten rule book. I never did that. I stuck to what I knew I was supposed to do. I felt that I was there to do a job and that there was a right way and a wrong way to do it. I understand that sometimes scouts go above and beyond by trying to find out about a player. They may talk to everyone and move around in the schools trying to get information on a guy. I just felt that was wrong. You have to be respectful when you go into schools, and I just thought that was disrespectful when scouts would do that, and at the end of the day almost all of that information was disclosed.

When you go to the schools enough, you make good contacts, and there are people there who you can rely on to get you the information that you need. You get to know people there who you can trust, people who will give you the straight scoop. I think at times there is a little overkill by scouts trying to get information kind of outside the lines. I felt that I was a guest at that particular university and I had to act like one.

I was a linebacker, but I didn't just evaluate linebackers. Every position takes a different set of skills. Every year we would have a scouting manual that we would go through. The position specifics did not change very often. The book was more of an administrative and informational tool, so the basics didn't change. When I started, all our scouts were veteran scouts. They had been around for a long time and knew what had to be done.

The process is basically the same but the gathering of information and technology have made the distribution of information lightning fast. What might have once taken a number of days to do is now available at the press of a button.

We all try to do the best we can and aim to never have a bad scouting report. What I mean by "bad" is twofold: either a good report on a bad player or a bad report on a good player. That said, it is impossible to measure the size of someone's heart or their passion for the game. You can have all of the measurables in the world on a player being at the top of the class and then they come to your team and end up a bust. How does that happen? Because you cannot measure their passion for the game. With those internal things missing, they fail— and as a result, you fail with them.

Those are the ones that really bother you a lot. You think you did everything right as far as grading their abilities, but they don't make it. And it happens all the time. Those are the players that you remember the most, much more so than the game changers, the Hall of Famers, and the greats.

When we have missed on players, it is usually because of their personality rather than their skills. They just don't have the right stuff mentally. They suffer emotionally rather than physically. We had this discussion time and time again and it still holds true. The player does not have the right constitution or the heart to make it. Now when I am involved with a player that we think is top-notch and will be here for a long time, I don't act alone. Numerous others take a look at each player and usually we have a consensus that a guy is special, a sure thing, destined to be a great player. When he doesn't make it, it hurts because you have spent so much time evaluating this guy and expect him to upgrade your roster and football team.

With a top player there will be as many as five to six reports just from the scouting staff. The coaches will look at him too, so there may be as many as 10 grades on a player. When everyone is on the same page with a certain guy, it is almost overkill, but we are trying our best to find out, *Is this guy for real?*

When we traded Randy Moss to Oakland, we tried hard to replace him. That was our first mistake, because it is hard to replace a player with Randy's ability. I recall one guy we drafted with our first pick; he had everything—at least we thought he did. I mean, this guy could run, catch the ball…he had all of the skill sets. But he was a complete bust. The game was just too big for him. He lacked the passion and heart to become a great player. He was a nice young guy and he felt bad that he could not contribute. He had some commitment issues to the game and it didn't work out for him or for us.

I recall another guy, a defensive end, who was also a first round pick. He never established himself as a solid prospect and had a long history of injuries. He lacked the passion and the heart for the game and ultimately didn't make it. We missed on him and it hurt for a long time.

I was the one in charge of the draft at that time and was ultimately responsible for it. But of course we also had a lot of good draft picks, great players and great people with big hearts and lots of passion for the game. People like Kevin Williams, E.J. Henderson, Chad Greenway, and Adrian Peterson were outstanding—as was, of course, Randy Moss. As bad as you feel about those guys you missed on, you feel as good about the excellent ones.

When a scout is hired or developed by a team, it does help when a person has a background with football. If they played or coached or have been around the game for an extended period of time, then at least they have a background and a foundation to build on. But it's not a prerequisite. The Vikings have a person named Kelly Kleine who works in the personnel office and she is absolutely outstanding—extremely talented and very smart. She evaluates players and has been doing that for some time now. She is excellent in what she does. She has been a tremendous help to Rick Spielman, our general manager, as well as to all of the other scouts. She is getting her feet wet in the business and has found a niche by doing a great job. All of the scouts on our staff except for Kelly have played the game, although Kelly is a total jock herself. So they all had a foundation to build on. We knew they knew a lot about the game from a personal standpoint.

Scouting is not for everybody, that's for sure. Mostly because it requires prolonged absences from families. There is some specialization. In the end it's like everything else. You have to have passion, strong work ethic, and dedication. The number one thing that leads to a scout not doing well or losing the job comes down to work ethic. It is just that simple. It's all about what kind of sacrifices you are willing to make to get the job done.

When I was on the road 9 or 10 months out of the year, I never had much downtime. You had to stay on top of your scouting reports or you would just get overwhelmed. If you had to write 50 to 75 reports over the course of the week, you couldn't afford to get behind. The really good players were easy to write up; it was the in-between players who were the toughest. The ones in the middle always take the most time. You might spend 30 to 45 minutes on a report, and if you have seven or eight reports to write that night and you type like I do, that's going to take some time.

I have never worked outside of the Vikings organization, but I would assume a strong work ethic is universal. Whether in the medical profession, education, or any other field of work, work ethic can make a person stand out or wither away. It is the people who get their hands dirty and are willing to do the legwork who succeed.

We would all have our performance evaluated, and when I was a director I would evaluate our staff. We had a great staff and I trusted them—and I think they trusted me. That level of trust is hard to come by at times, but we had it. Trust is always important. We had to have it with the schools we visited. I had to trust the people I came in contact with. They would be essential to what I did every day. When I finished my job at one school and did the reports that night, the next day it was on to the next school and the next reports.

The longest I would be gone from home was two weeks. Our GM, Rick Spielman, felt we had to keep in regular touch with our families and encouraged us to get home as often as we could. Some scouts would be gone longer, and you would admire their dedication to their work, but it is important to get away from the job every once in a while, and we owed it to ourselves and our families.

The job also got expensive for the team. Although that was not a huge factor, it was something that was watched to some extent. Being on the road six to eight weeks can rachet up the costs. Scouts are under a lot of stress, and it is important that they get home once in a while and kick their feet up, while also keeping some of the costs down.

Living on the road can be expensive. We stayed in a lot of hotels. The NFL had a deal with the Marriott, so most of the time I stayed at a Marriott property. Each of our scouts had a car allowance, so we would drive our own vehicles and get reimbursed for mileage. It was added income for us. I always drove a truck or a Suburban or a Tahoe—I liked having a large vehicle around me when I was traveling all over the country.

Some guys drive their whole area. And while scouting directors fly to certain areas, they all spend a considerable amount of time in rental cars and on airplanes. I loved working in the Midwest, and I got to know the people and those schools well.

Jamaal Stephenson, who is our scouting director now, covers the entire country. Although with COVID-19 out there, no one is traveling now. I do believe I would have a tough time adjusting to today's climate.

There is a lot of cross-checking during the scouting process, and by draft time there aren't many stones unturned. Rick Spielman is a top-notch evaluator and spends countless hours watching both pro and college players.

As a scout, I saw a lot of film, but I didn't go to a lot of football games on Saturdays. I know that sounds a little strange, but I had a good reason and made up for it in other ways. I had a problem going to the games and evaluating players. I don't know what it is, but when you go to a game you might have to look at several players. You might be scouting a defensive back and a guard or tackle and at the same time be looking at a wide receiver. I had a hard time watching, focusing, and separating all of the different positions simultaneously. Sometimes you might have a dozen prospects to watch. I just couldn't follow everyone. I followed the ball! I couldn't go from receiver to running back to defensive back. I never felt that I missed anything, though, by not seeing those games in person. For me, it was best to watch players on tape. I could then concentrate on what I was supposed to do and not get caught up in the game.

I did attend a lot of practices. When you were at a school you were basically there for the whole day, so practices were a part of it. I liked my schedule and what it called for me to do. There is no question, though, that it was a lot of work.

When I became director, my responsibilities got increased quite a bit. Fortunately, I was also able to hire some great people. They are all still there today, and I feel really good about that. It's a different blend of characters who all get along with each other and do a great job.

Our scouts with the Vikings are:

- College Director: Jamaal Stephenson
- National Scouts: Mike Sholiton, Pat Roberts
- Area Scouts: Frank Acevedo, Sean Gustus, Kevin McCabe, Chisom Opara, Conrad Cardano, Blaine Gramer, Jake Essler (BLESTO), Kelly Kleine
- Director of Pro Scouting: Ryan Monnens
- Assistant Pro Director: Reed Burckhardt
- Player Personnel Consultant: Paul Wiggin
- Director of Analytics/Pro Scout: Scott Kuhn

The thing I liked the most about the job was being around the game. To be able to work in a business that you loved as a player was really something. I could not have asked for a better job. To me, the best job in football is playing. Probably the next-best is coaching, even though job security isn't there, and the next-best job is scouting.

I was very lucky to have been a player for 14 years and a scout for 28 years, all with the Minnesota Vikings. Being a part of the football business is special. We worked hard to get the best players in trying to build a championship team.

It was difficult to be away from home so much, but I was dedicated. I wouldn't say the job was overwhelming, but it was stressful—especially when the draft rolls around. You are picking players for the team's future and you hope you are right. When you make a draft pick, you will soon find out if you made the right decision. It's just one of those things; you never really know until they get out on the field and show you that they are the right kind of guys that can help you contend for an NFL championship (or not). But it was always an exciting part of the job, seeing them on the field wearing our uniforms.

The cycle of the scouting department runs about 10 months a year. Our scouts are able to decompress in the summertime, but it is still a year-round job. Today scouts have lost the ability to stay away completely because they may be grading guys at different points during the summer months. You go like hell for 9 or 10 months and transition into the fall season, when you are evaluating players all day every day until the college season ends. Then you are cross-checking your positions and going to All-Star games and going to the NFL Combine and doing your spring work.

Then there are the juniors, who are declaring for the draft more and more every year. That increases the workload quite a bit, but you kind of get into a groove so that you know the times of the year when the workload will be heavy. And you also know what time of the year it will not be as heavy.

The No. 1 skill for an NFL scout is having direct knowledge of the game. This can come from playing the game, coaching it, or being around it. The majority of the people in this profession have one of those backgrounds. Maybe it wasn't a football background but an athletic background, but they know what it takes to perform at a certain level, succeed at a certain level, what it takes to be a good teammate, and other things related to the game.

In order to evaluate talent, you have to have a certain aptitude for it. And as I say time and again, you have to have a very strong work ethic. You have to be willing to go the extra mile to get the job done. This might be going on the road, watching extra tape, talking to as many resources as you can in order to get a feel for an individual player, and having the overall skill to evaluate talent.

To succeed, you have to have a dedication to your craft. Whether you are a player, a coach, a scout, or a GM, it's trying to be the best that you can be by not leaving any stones unturned. It is the willingness to get your hands dirty while doing the work. You either have it or you don't, although I do believe you can improve upon it.

A big part of the job is the ability to accept the fact that you will be wrong at times. But as long as you feel good about your day and left nothing out, there is some satisfaction. You should be able to walk away from a school on a given day and have a good feeling for its players without second-guessing yourself. If you are wrong you are wrong, but if that's your opinion, that's what they pay you for—and that's what counts in the end.

A good scout strives to be right, and it's important to have conviction. There are a number of times when everyone is on the same page and feels good about a certain player and you still miss. It is those intangibles that are so hard to measure. Until the player is your property you will never know.

Some players walk in the door with it and some never get it. Sometimes guys have to get cut a couple times before they figure it out. When you pick a player in the draft, you certainly hope you are right even though you never know for sure at the time.

We always have players about whom the scouts have different opinions. I might have watched a player play three games early in the season and other scouts may have watched that same player later in the season against different competition. That player's level of success may have peaked or gone down over the course of the season. That's when you have to go back and reevaluate what you thought at the time. Sometimes we would do a "group study" as a staff. What was the difference in competition at the times when they were evaluated? Did you know that the kid was banged up for two or three games? Did he have family problems going on that may have distracted him for two or three weeks?

There are so many different variables going on that can affect a player, and it is really important to consider all of the factors when developing the final report. This requires going back over the player to be sure you know every single thing that was going on in his life throughout the season. Maybe he was a first-year starter or a late bloomer. Maybe he got better as the season went along. You have to protect your opinion at all times, but maybe you will have to go back and reevaluate the player and your opinion will change. Looking and evaluating just once will not always work.

Eventually you will see what other scouts will say about your player, especially with the top prospects. You try to evaluate as many as you can on a daily and weekly basis. When I was director, I might have graded 800 to 900 players in an average year, enough to have a good feel for the draft board—and I know Jamaal Stephenson feels the same way. That's a lot of players, a lot of reports, and a lot of work. That's how I knew I was doing the best job for the team. Not every player I did an evaluation for was a top player; many of them were seen as middle- or late-round players or possible free agents. You have to have a feel for the *entire* draft board.

Of course, you could never get to everyone, so you just had to cut it off where you felt it was best. There is a big difference between the top guys and the bevy of free agents. But free agents are important too. Adam Theilen of the Vikings is a perfect example of that. You never have the time to be able to go through the entire free agent list and pick the gems out of there, but you give it your best shot and sometimes you get lucky.

When Mike Tice was our offensive line coach, he and I worked out Matt Birk because he was a local guy who had a great Ivy League career. He wasn't a high draft choice and was a work in progress, but he sure played well for us (and later, Baltimore). He was extremely intelligent, athletic, and a great player for a long time in the league.

Scouting is not rocket science by a long shot. A person is going to make mistakes and have hits and misses along the way. It's a crap shoot at best when you are dealing with people—who have different moods and feelings and temperaments—but to get the best scouting reports, using sound judgment and measurables will certainly help.

Again, it is very hard to judge the size of someone's heart. You really don't have anything that can measure that other than what you see, feel, and what you think about players when you see them on tape, in person, or through talking to contacts at the school. Do they have what it takes to play at this level? What is it about them that makes them special?

Ultimately, I left the scouting director position because I got burned out. For me it was the right time to step down. I needed a break from the daily grind of the director's job. I enjoyed it very much and liked the challenge, but the responsibilities were enormous, and I had done the job for many years.

As far as I know there wasn't any problem with my performance; neither Rick nor George Paton, who is now GM for the Denver Broncos, had any trouble with my work. It was just time for a change. It was totally my decision and they were very supportive of it. I cannot be more grateful as to how I was treated and how they assisted me through the change. I went from the director of scouting back to an area scout. I remained very heavily involved in all aspects of the scouting area.

Once I finally decided to retire for good, it was, again, just time. I still enjoyed the process, the workload, the people…all the aspects of the job. It was one of the hardest things to walk away from. But I owed it to my family and I owed it to myself. It is not very often that a person can spend 42 years in this business with the same organization. I retired in three different ways: as a player, as director, and as a scout. It was a phenomenal run.

I have had no second thoughts about retirement. I thank my lucky stars every day for the career I had. Someone has been watching over me, that's for sure.

Retirement is a work in progress, but I don't miss the grind. I do miss the people. But that is always true when you have a job that you thoroughly enjoy. I made the right decision and it has been good for the family, and me too.

CHAPTER EIGHT

The NFL Draft

The NFL Draft is a heavily concentrated nine-months-a-year process. Typically the out-of-town guys have some time off in the summer months. Once training camp starts they all come to camp to get their schedules ready and evaluate our roster. (Although this year, I was told the staff was working more than usual over the summer months. They were asked to evaluate all of the A and B players in order to get a feel for the upcoming draft class.) Scouts depart camp after about a week to 10 days and then go on their merry way, visiting their schools.

Because of COVID-19, the majority of scouts are staying at home and working from there. If I were still scouting, I know I would be totally frustrated. This time of the year normally you are accustomed to being on the road. The scouts will have all the background information available, and most of their connections have remained at the schools in their area, but access this year will be limited. They will have to film-grade the players instead of seeing them in person. I suspect it will be very hard on the scouts; I think I retired at the right time.

Because the Vikings are a member of BLESTO they have an initial rating chart by position and by school that contains all of the prospects. They get all that information in the spring, so teams have a good idea about how to get their work done. All the major programs are pretty much the same year in and year out. It's the small schools with a prospect that need to be accounted for.

College free agents are stacked and reevaluated in the spring, and there are always a number of players that move up on your board and become potential draft candidates. A player may have one grade going into the school, but you generally end up with three or four looks when players move up the board.

Rick Spielman likes going into the schools to take a look at players. He likes to see a lot of them. The list of prospects always grows as you get more into the scouting season, and there is just a tremendous amount of information available to the teams. Everyone who is a draft prospect is looked at.

Today it is very naive to think you can slip somebody through that no one has looked at. There is so much information out there on the players, it is almost impossible. Player scouting is the lifeblood of professional football. The draft is the focus of every professional football team and their way of maintaining and improving their roster. Back when I started some 28 years ago plenty of things were different, but the bottom line was still the same: we used every means possible to find the best players for the football team and keep a step up on our competition.

I know the Vikings are very thorough. They are very focused on the top guys available but they are also very focused on the bottom pieces. There are a lot of players who are lower-round draft choices who turn out to be great pro players.

Preparing for the draft takes a great deal of time and effort. It is a very thorough process, and Rick and George, as well as many others in the organization, are great examples of what it takes. With the Vikings, it is not very often that a player will slip through the cracks, and Rick always goes above and beyond when it comes to personnel.

During a typical draft the Vikings may pick eight or nine players, and although it differs from year to year, typically your front board may have around 250 players on it. Some teams only have as few as 100 but we have a large number. It's the number that we feel that we need to make the best possible picks. There are always enough players to pick from, but we want to be sure the ones on our list are the right ones. At some point during the season there will be more than a thousand names on our board, simply accounting for everyone. Once we get through what we would call our back board or college free agent stack, we typically don't go back to it.

Now, there are some players who do something in the spring, at the Combine, or maybe heal up from an injury who will get another look. But by the time the draft rolls around, we have not missed anybody and have comprehensive information on the draft class. Perhaps we have devalued a particular player, maybe we need to get another look at him, but we do know about him. By the time you get to the draft all the work has been done and it is time to focus on the players who you think will come in and help your team most.

Our IT department is heavily involved, along with our analytics department, in putting the board together. We have excellent people who do an outstanding job. Everything is electronic now, so it makes it so much easier. With the push of a button, you can bring up any list or person you want. It is way beyond my pay grade, that's for sure. I found that our people were always there for us when we needed them, and they all add a lot of value to the draft process.

Because of my lack of technology skills, I always appreciated the assistance that this group provided. They can do miracles with this kind of stuff! The support staff is huge, and they make sure that things run the way the general manager wants them to run. In particular, I would like to acknowledge Paul Nelson, Luke Burson, and Scott Kuhn, our analytics directors, for their great work.

When we are preparing for the draft, the college scouting staff, pro staff, and coaching staff all get involved, as well as our trainers and medical staff. It is all very amicable. Everybody's opinion is valued, and only one opinion overrides most of them, and that's Rick's. He sees all the players, as does Jamal. There is usually somewhat of a consensus formed, with one person accountable for the way the players are stacked. If there is disagreement, it is hashed out. The bottom line is that everybody gets a say, but after all the opinions are in, Rick makes the final decision. Everyone in the organization respects everyone else and it works exceptionally well.

Once the draft begins, we have one board that stacks players by position and another board that rates the players by value, from the first pick to the last pick—an overall ranking by players and by position, respectively.

Rick likes to trade and move around on draft weekend. And he likes to have a certain number of picks for the year. He is always looking to move around in the draft. Admittedly, it used to drive me crazy—it was kind of a standing joke at our place. But I get it. I understand it and I respect it, although I didn't necessarily like it all the time.

Mike Zimmer is very much engaged in the whole draft process, but he does not get directly involved in picking the players on draft day. Rick knows what kind of player Mike wants and Zim understands how it all works. They have a great relationship and let one another do their respective jobs. They have discussions on the side about what kind of people they want for certain positions and they work really well together. Mike is a football coach and is frankly more interested in the players he has; he leaves the draft pretty much to Rick. He is hands-on, but not to the extent that some other coaches are.

Zimmer used to ask, "Are we ever going to pick a player, or are we going to just keep trading back?" Rick likes to have a lot of options, and that's fine, but it took me a while to buy into everything he does. But now I believe in it—and he does a great job. That's the way he wants to do things and he is the man in charge. You have to respect him for it. It's not necessarily the way I would do it, but it's the way he does it and that's okay with me. I get it. There are always options on draft weekend, and I guess I used to think if there is a player there that you wanted, just take him rather than move around trying to pick up additional draft choices along the way. But it works for Rick, and I respect him for it. It serves him well, so more power to him.

When we are ready to go on draft day, there are a lot of people in the room. There are the personnel people, the scouting people, the head coach, the offensive and defensive coordinators, a position coach—occasionally, to talk about a particular player—the IT people, the owners, the general manager and top assistants, the salary cap vice president, Rob Brzezinski, and others.

It's a very busy room, but everything has been hashed out over the course of weeks and months. The plan is in place for the coming three days. It is a very quiet, well-organized room. There is a lot of waiting around, but it is *our* game day. It is a very stressful time for everyone—especially as you get closer to your pick. It is exciting, rewarding, and unpredictable, to say the least—good and bad. But it is a wonderful experience. It's what you work toward for nine months, and it all boils down to three days.

College free agency comes right after the draft, so it makes for a very busy time. But as I say, it's a very rewarding experience. The draft is something I will never forget. I was involved in 28 of them, and every one was extraordinary and different.

There is very little said during the draft. Everybody, as I have said, has had a chance to say their piece and get it all out in the open beforehand, so on draft day, very little is spoken in the room. Rick has his plan in place so the conversations are kept to a minimum. If someone needs to have a private conversation, then they leave the room. This would only involve a few select people. The scouts are basically done with their work, so they're rarely involved in these side conversations. Everybody respects that and understands that. It is a good group; everybody knows their place and accepts it.

Over the years there have been quite a few changes in the draft. Today, the popularity is incredible. It has grown into a highly rated event. It is an absolute televised spectacular, and one of the highlights of the National Football League calendar. People live and die for the NFL Draft. There are people that absolutely can't wait for the draft. For us it is all business. It is the culmination of a lot of hard work, so it's typically a rewarding weekend for the scouting department. Once it finally happens and it's over with, you want to decompress for a few days.

There's a lot of pressure, just as there is with the baseball, basketball, and hockey drafts. It is a big deal—it is the culmination of a lot of hard work designed to improve your team. It is the lifeblood of your football team.

Today, with so much turnover on the rosters, it has become even more important. Rosters change almost daily. In 2020, with all of the injuries early in the season, rosters were just devastated by injured guys who could not be replaced. For some teams, the draft is not their centerpiece, but for others it is. Replacing players who get injured cannot always be through the draft.

The draft can never be personal. Everybody has their favorites, guys who you would stand on the table and yell out for, but at the end of the day, it is the Minnesota Vikings' draft. At the end of the day, it is our picks, not my picks—not Rick's picks, but the Vikings' picks, and we all stand by it.

We believe the players drafted are the kind of players who we want walking into our building every day. We hope that the guys selected are the kind of players and people who will make us better and compete for a championship. That's really all that matters at the end of the day. It doesn't matter if it's my guy or Rick's guy; it's *our* guy. You won't be successful without that kind of a philosophy.

We generally send two people from our scouting department to the NFL headquarters to officially give the card to the commissioner or his representative for each draft pick. They get the pick from the team and turn it in to the commissioner or the podium. Once a player is picked, he is called and congratulated, and has a short conversation with several of our personnel. Those people include Rick Spielman, our GM; Mike Zimmer, our head coach; the offensive or defensive coordinator; a position coach; and then eventually they would get in touch with the people in operations to set a schedule for possibly a visit or minicamp that next weekend. (It's a little different now. Remember my call when I was drafted?)

Rick always makes the final decision, and for the most part we all know who he is going to pick before he does it. There are no secrets inside the room. Rick has always been very transparent with all of the scouts. We were never kept in the dark, and we appreciated that very much.

Sometimes during the draft, things can change dramatically and you might have to go in a different direction, but even with that, we have always been on board with what the team decides to do. The consensus is very strong in that room. Everybody has everyone else's back—it has to be that way if you want it to work. The team ownership is in the draft room. They are very interested in what we do, but they don't offer opinions about how we do things or why we are doing them. I know Rick keeps them informed as to which way we may go. They understand that this is our expertise and they are comfortable with that, which, again, is greatly appreciated. They let the people in the room do their jobs and offer a great deal of support. It has been an ideal situation. That kind of mutual respect is why it works and why I stayed with it all these years.

The NFL Draft used to be 15 rounds and then 12 and now it is down to 7. That's a lot of players who may be good football players who do not get drafted. I think it is good to some extent but it puts a lot of pressure on teams to go after the free agents after the draft is over. When there were 15 rounds, and then 12, it solidified more players with more teams. But then the days were longer and the workload was similar. I like it the way it is now, with seven rounds. The downside is that it doesn't allow teams to secure the number of players they could before. Therefore the competition is greater to land the free agent, especially that coveted free agent.

I like the system the way it is. I mentioned before that Rick is a huge proponent of draft picks and he likes to move around during the draft and secure as many picks as he can. He strives for perfection all the time, and the draft is a way for him to make an impact on the Vikings football team. He is excellent at his craft.

When the Vikings make a trade it is based on a point chart. Rob Brzezinski and Rick are the keys to everything involving our football team. They are the ones that make all the phone calls before and during the draft to various clubs, to see if they are willing to move back in the draft or jump ahead.

Every pick in the draft is assigned a point value, so when a trade is considered you can look at the point value and see if they match up. In order to make it a fair trade, the point charts have to be close to equal and the point charts related to the draft number of the pick.

Every draft pick was assigned a point value, so when you considered a trade on draft day, you would look at the picks and see what the point values equaled. This was a way to determine if you were making a fair trade, and is a good tool to lean on. I was not directly involved in any of this kind of maneuvering. Rick has huge contacts around the league and is comfortable in making these decisions and willing to roll the dice at times.

After the draft the Vikings start signing free agents, and it is a mad scramble. You are not supposed to talk to these players before the draft is over, but it does happen. A lot of these deals are made under the table, and by the time the draft is over some of these players are already signed, sealed, and delivered. But that's not the way it's supposed to work.

We would list players as A, B, and C prospects, and then sign them and pay them accordingly. We have found some pretty good players out of free agency over the years, so it's an important piece of the puzzle for us. The best players available are coveted after the draft. Each scout has a position coach that he works with. The coaches would call players and recruit them, try to get a feel for where they are now, where they were and who they were talking to, and see if they were available and free to sign.

We always felt that when we offered them a contract it was an opportunity for them to show us what they've got, a chance to see if they could make our football team. Some of them would go for the money, some would go by the depth at their position with a given team. Generally player agents are involved, and that makes it difficult in some cases. Our goal was always to give a player a chance who we felt actually had a chance to make the team or practice squad.

The majority of those slots were filled right after the draft, but there were always a few positions that were left open to be filled when you had time to circle back to your board on Sunday.

It's tough on the teams, the players, their families, and it is a very trying few days figuring out what to do that's best for your football team. It's worse, though, for the player who expected to be drafted and then wasn't. The important thing is for those players to never give up, because there are a lot of players who fall into that category and then sign as free agents and play for a long time in the league. They don't get first-round money or second-round money, but if they end up making the club they will make some pretty good money the first year and then go from there.

Just take a look at Johnny Randle. Here is a guy who went undrafted and came to camp and just shined from day one. He was 245 pounds, with a motor that never quit. Keith Millard was there at under tackle, so he wasn't going to take his place. But Johnny came in as a tireless worker with an unbelievable passion for the game. He did not have a huge impact that first year, but he was so quick and tenacious and had all the intangibles—except the size.

He became a force later on at 290 pounds that could not be blocked. He was relentless. He wanted to make it so bad that he just never gave up. He did exceptionally well for himself, and that's Johnny. We missed on Johnny early on but struck gold later on. He showed everyone what he was made of, and now he is in the Pro Football Hall of Fame. Again, you cannot measure a guy's heart, and Johnny's was as big as anyone's.

After the draft is over and the players come in for minicamp and OTAs, I would go out and watch them, see what they look like, how they act, and how they stack up against the others. I was always interested in their personalities, how they fit, what they were like, and the kind of skill set they brought. The fact is, though, they don't make the team in May or June. They make it in July, August, and September.

CHAPTER NINE

The Scout's Calendar

When we start preparing for the draft we have two scouts who basically split the country in half as regional or national scouts, along with seven area scouts and our BLESTO scout. We then have Rick and others who are very important in what we are trying to accomplish on draft day and who are on top of the whole scouting staff.

If the most important part of your job is what you like to do the most, you have it made. I absolutely loved scouting. I enjoyed the challenge, being out on the road, and being in different schools. Every single day was different. You might go into a school and be pleasantly surprised based on the information that you had going in. Maybe there were better players at the school than you previously thought, or maybe you go into a school that has a bunch of highly rated players but you walk away disappointed.

The challenge was doing the work, watching the tapes of the players and watching practice. It would always depend on the day you were there and the time of the year; that made every day so very different. Every day was challenging and unpredictable. The challenge was to identify the talent to the best of your ability and then you move on to the next school. Every day you started over.

A lot of times the days begin to run together. It makes it harder to start separating the guys until you get away from it for a bit. You need time in order to refresh yourself. There were times when the grind would get to me as I went into the fall months, but it was never something I couldn't handle. There is an old saying in scouting when evaluating a player: "If they can't play in September they are sure not going to be able to play in November." But you may also have to put a disclaimer on that statement. As you go through the fall you will find that some of the players will be better than you thought and some will grade out worse than you thought. You almost had to start over on the same class at the end of November and after the all-star games were over. So at that point you take a deep breath and begin again. It really comes down to two different seasons and approaches for the scouts.

That gives you the ability in the spring and winter months to go back through the players that you evaluated and make sure that you were correct in your analysis of them. Getting them right in your evaluations is important, and that gave you the opportunity to double-check yourself and your work.

As a scout, there was never a part of the job that I didn't like. It was such a unique position, and it almost had a fraternity feel to it. It is a position that allows you to make a lot of friends with staff from other teams, the schools, coaches, and so many other arenas. I had the opportunity to make connections all over the country. You would typically run into other scouts at schools; it was very rare that you were in a school by yourself. There were generally scouts and other people that you enjoyed being around. Sure, you would also occasionally run into some that maybe you didn't get along with as well, but mostly they were good people with the same goals. Great friendships were formed.

There was a challenge in all of the travel that you had to do, and the evaluations were critical. Writing reports on all that you observed during the days made for a lot of long days and long nights. I would say that was the most tiresome thing. If you didn't stay up with them then you started to fall behind fast. Once you get to piling on school after school and player after player, if you don't keep up with the workload, stress and panic come.

Rick wanted the reports sent in every week so he could monitor where the prospects were. With that in mind, you can see what can happen if you don't keep up. We always had deadlines that the scouts would have to meet. There were times where we might have had personal or family problems and you had to try and keep the right balance. The Vikings have always been very supportive in those instances, and when it happens it is family first—and has always been that way. It was a good feeling to always know that we had the backing of Rick and the ownership. It was clear that they knew that all of their scouts were conscientious people who would get the work done. Life does get in the way sometimes, and the team has always been very understanding in that regard.

When you evaluate a good player there are always things that set him apart. There are so many ingredients that combine to make a good player—how they tick and how they work and the kinds of things they do are all a part of it. A lot of the things that make somebody a good player are things that you just cannot measure. Their passion for the game, as I have said before, the kind of heart that you are looking for, the kind of mindset that you are looking for—those are all things that you cannot coach.

All these traits typically show up in their play, the way they interact with their teammates, the way they are on the sideline, the way they are on game day, and more. When you go into a school, you can always find glowing reports about a player's intangibles, along with some lukewarm reports of the same. Some guys just have it and some don't; it is something that cannot be taught. That kind of stuff is inherent in their personalities, and it typically shows on a regular practice day and on game day. I know that I had it, and I tried very hard to find it in others. Talking about the intangibles could fill an entire book, they're so important. I can't help myself.

The more people that confirm a player's desire to be great, the better. It may be head coach, coordinator, position coach, strength coach, trainer, or anyone else who knows the person. This type of individual meets them all by being one of the first on the field and one of the last off it. These are the guys who are always working on their game, the ones who hold themselves and their teammates accountable. They just simply stand out in a crowd. Whether they quietly lead by example or are vocal in what they do, those guys typically stand out. Is it desire? Is it heart? Is it both? Who knows for sure—maybe a little (or a lot) of each.

I think one of the things you have to do as a scout—or in any profession, really—is self-evaluate. It's when you make a mistake that you try to find ways to do it better. Now, if you are constantly making mistakes and not trying to find a way to get better, you won't be scouting in the league very long. You have to be self-critical and go back to determine what you missed in a particular player. As I said before, it's the guys that you miss who are hardest to forget and who haunt you.

Sometimes when players fail, it's just that the NFL is too big for them. They can't handle the competition or the pressure; they fall by the wayside and get gobbled up by the system. They just can't keep up. It does happen, and it's just the way it goes. In fact, it happens in every business and in every industry. The cream rises to the top, they say, and sometimes, for whatever reason, people don't have the mental fortitude to handle it and stay up.

The majority of these players are fairly well prepared for the next step beyond their collegiate careers. They played in grade school, they played in high school, and they played in college, and now they are ready for professional football. They have gone through all the steps both mentally and physically, so they should be ready for that next step. But for some, somewhere along the way, they are missing something. They have been competing all their lives, so when they get to an NFL camp as a draft pick or as a free agent, they have earned their place to be there. But a lot of times, there are players ahead of them who are just better than they are, and they're just not talented enough to make it. Now, that's not to say that they can't go somewhere else and make it. It happens all the time, more frequently than you would like to admit.

Sometimes the environment is just not right for them, then they go somewhere else and make it. The depth at the position makes it tough. I'm sure that in the 2020 COVID-19 year it was extremely hard to evaluate players and cut down the roster with no preseason games and a minimal amount of live contact in practice. The preseason games give the rookies a chance to make the team and establish themselves. I'm sure that some players didn't get a real chance at all, due to the limited amount of time that they practiced and/or the limited amount of reps. There may not have been enough time for teams to get a real feel for the players—but I wasn't there, so I am just speculating.

The scouts during COVID-19 are doing their jobs at home rather than on the road, and I'd guess it probably doesn't sit real well. My guess is they would say they like being out there around the players, the schools, and the coaches. It is important to be in the schools doing your job to really get a feel for the players. You have got to be around them in order to feel good about the evaluations that you make on these players. Everything is virtual these days, but I think that the rank-and-file members in the scouting departments would prefer to be on the road because they like being out there where you get to evaluate film at the schools and get to talk with all of your contacts about a player. There is something to be said about face-to-face contact, watching players live and in person, and talking face-to-face with the staff and coaches. It is a huge part of scouting, and although it is tiring and extremely cumbersome at times, I believe it is necessary. Having your hands on the players, so to speak, and talking to your school contacts, along with watching the players interact with their teammates—that's all critical and enhances the reports that you write.

You don't get that personal touch when you are just watching tape at home. Communication is so much better in person and the way you evaluate is clearer. Even with the COVID-19 year that we have had, the school contacts are critical. They're the bread and butter of scouting.

In the 28 years that I was in scouting I learned a great deal. The people I was so fortunate to be around both as a player and as a scout were instrumental in my development in both areas. You start with Bud and with Burnsie, and then go to the scouting side with Frank

Gilliam and Jerry Reichow—who had been in the industry forever—and a very veteran scouting staff with Conrad Cardano, Don Deisch, Ralph Kohl, and Johnny Carson. I learned so much from the people mentioned. I think you have to have a certain amount of respect for the game, and if you do, it all works out in the end. As long as you have that and attain that, you have a chance to be successful.

I believe that no matter what your job, there is a commonsense approach. The commonsense approach works the same whether you are scouting or selling insurance or working in a gas station. It's learning about the right way to do it, the way that makes good sense. As you learn this over time, the job becomes easier. Unfortunately, the job gets harder to some extent because as the years go by, you get older and don't have the same amount of energy.

I learned so much about life from Bud. He was so observant; he never missed a trick. As a young player, I never said two words to Bud—and he didn't say two words to me either. He was aloof to the point where he was almost intimidating, but that was just his style. He taught me so much as a player and as a scout but more so than that about people and about life—how to live it and be successful.

He kept to himself for the most part, but you just knew that he was on top of his business by the way he conducted himself both on and off the field. He had interests other than football, but he had a great command and a great feel as to how to manage his team. And there was never any doubt that it was his football team. Even today, every time I talk to Bud, everything he says makes so much sense. A friend of mine once told me that when Bud comes into your office and has a talk with you, when he leaves it feels like you have just completed a five-credit course.

Bud rarely raised his voice. I think I may have heard him raise his voice once, but I'm not sure of that either. He was a very emotional person but never showed it. I know that he cared about people. He was very successful and he was very passionate, one of those guys who didn't have to say a lot to get his point across.

The way Bud approached the business was unique. He just had such a commonsense approach to everything. It's not rocket science. The game is surely more complicated than the way it used to be, but Bud could handle it then and could handle it today. He would probably be the first one to tell you that if you have a lot of great players, then you have a chance. I think he probably realized that a long time ago. Dependability was such a huge focus of his. Knowing what you were going to get from a particular player week in and week out was paramount in Bud's philosophy.

Jerry Burns was one of the great characters in the business. He was the offensive coordinator while he was an assistant coach, and I was on the other side of the ball, so I never had a lot of contact with him. But once he became the head coach that changed. He was very creative as a coach and extremely consistent. He was very passionate about the game and the game was very important to him. I loved playing for Jerry. He was a friend as well as the head coach. I didn't want to let him down. He was a great role model like Bud was, and I became a better person because of him. The way Burnsie handled himself and the way he was really in touch with his players had an effect on me. I tried to be a lot like him and Bud in my own way. Both Bud and Jerry had so much to offer, and yet they could not have been more different personality-wise. The two of them had unique qualities about them that made them both excellent head coaches. I was fortunate to play for them and get to know them both so well. It served me well. Above all, it was their personalities that really rubbed off on me.

When I did my job, it was paramount to me to have my bosses be able to count on me all the time for everything. My dependability on the football field and in the scouting offices was essential to me. I wanted to have Rick and others know that they could always count on me, just like I did when I was playing for Bud and Burnsie. The majority of the people in this business are self-starters because if you aren't, you won't last. At the end of the day, you have to be accountable for what you are doing. If you're not, people are going to see right through you and you won't make it.

One of the big days on the scouting calendar is the NFL Combine. It is held during every off-season in Indianapolis, and it has grown into quite an event over the years. It has turned into a well-oiled machine and is very organized. It is a great venue for these players to be in front of 32 teams. And it's a chance for the teams to see all of the top prospects in one place. We would have a BLESTO meeting at the Combine to go over the juniors who had declared for the draft. We would interview players, watch the workouts, and most importantly get extensive medical information on the players, all of which amounted to long days and busy nights.

Quite honestly, I was never a huge fan of the Combine. I always felt that its most important aspect was the medical part. The medical information that we received was absolutely critical. You could get the information ahead of time from the schools and the trainers, but the doctors had the opportunity to put their hands on the players and they had the ability to run a wide variety of tests and scans to rule out a potential problem or red-flag a particular medical condition.

There are a lot of medical findings that pop up at the Combine that you may not have known about from your school call. A red flag can often pop up. It is unfortunate for some of the players, but it is something that is absolutely critical for teams to know. You have to know if there is a medical risk with any of these players and you may end up steering clear of that particular prospect.

They have examination stations at the stadium and the players rotate in and out of exam rooms. All the information that we would gather was shared somewhat, but it was more on our doctors and training staff to determine what they found. It is a very important part of the process, and it is something that teams spend a lot of time and money on. It is necessary to avoid mistakes with players. Eric Sugarman, his staff, and all our medical staff do a great job with their evaluations and compiling information.

The players are invited to the Combine by a committee of personnel departments from the NFL. I'm not sure how they select this committee. The Combine is run by Jeff Foster and his staff, and he does a phenomenal job. He originally had some club affiliation, and was in the scouting profession, but now running the Combine is a full-time job. The Combine has always been in Indianapolis. I know there has been some talk about changing the venue, but I'm not sure if that's going to happen. The league is heavily involved in the process as well, and all I would say is, if it ain't broke, don't fix it.

For me the on-field activity doesn't always tell you what you want to know about a player. The workout may tell you about someone and what they can do as far as their speed, their ability to bench press so much weight, jump so high, or any number of other things, but it does not tell you how they are going to play on Sunday afternoon.

As soon as the season is over, players start training for the Combine. They go to speed coaches and strength coaches, things like that, in preparation. And they come up with some surprising numbers. But the only guys they can't fool are the medical people.

They are not in pads, and work out in regular gym clothes, but it can enhance a player's stock if he puts up good numbers and is a good player on tape. Some guys go to the Combine and just blow it up, do a sensational job. Numbers-wise they show a lot of potential, but when you scout the player you don't see those numbers in practice or in games. So it is not an exact science by any stretch of the imagination. I think a lot of times if you get sold on the height, weight, and speed of a player, you may make a mistake.

There are about 325 players invited to the Combine every year. Without question it is every player's goal to get the invite; that is a benchmark for the NFL. Still, there are a lot of guys who don't get invited but still make a team. Maybe they fall through the cracks because they are a small-school guy or had an injury-prone season or didn't play that much. They can't bring everybody, so some players have to get their chance through their Pro Day or by other means.

Pro Day is when a school has a day for NFL people to come in and test their players. There are always guys that pop up and get an opportunity to show what they have. If the guy comes from your scouting area, you need to get a report on the guy and account for him. You just cannot afford to miss anybody, because the word will get out.

Take a guy like Adam Thielen, wide receiver for the Vikings out of Mankato State. He had a Pro Day and was what we call an "unwritten player." He went to one of the regional Combines, which follow the NFL Combine, and he worked out well there. Our pro scouts were there at the time, and Ryan Monnens, our pro director, liked what he saw. Thielen ran pretty well, caught the ball well, had decent size and graded out as a prospect.

We invited him to our rookie minicamp after the draft. We didn't expect much from Adam even though he did test pretty well in several areas. He showed up at our minicamp and ultimately we decided to sign him to our active roster. He was a practice squad player the first year and a special teamer the second year. Adam continued to grow as a player and he turned into a great player for us.

The majority of the schools have a Pro Day. Some of the smaller schools may team up with other schools, but they all try to give their players an opportunity to be seen by professional scouts. There are a lot of different opportunities for every player to get a look if they want one. It's one way for the school to showcase their potential draft class, and the sessions are very well attended by scouts from the NFL.

It is a huge circuit in the spring, with Pro Days going on all over the country every day. Every Pro Day is different depending on the school. You could have six or seven players show up in one place and then you go into another school or group of schools and 18 show up. It varies considerably. Each player wants to do something special to get on some NFL team's board or radar and get a chance at playing professional football. These guys have worked hard for four or five years and this is their shot.

After the Combine, we would meet with all of the scouting staff and finalize what our plan was for the upcoming draft. We would follow up and do more work on certain players and attend a number of Pro Days. Preparing for the draft was critical, and we would spend countless hours getting ready for it.

With the number of players involved and all the work that needed to be done on each one, I did feel overwhelmed at times, even if I was just broken down for a short time. During the height of the season, with all that had to be done, there wasn't time to take off, so the burden of the work was extremely taxing at times. We always felt it was important for our guys to decompress after the draft, so we all got some time off at this point. I know the Vikings organization felt strongly that the time off was needed as well, and that coming back ready to go was important. From the end of the draft and through May and June, our college staff were basically on their own until training camp started again in the summer.

I never really aspired to be a general manager, but there was a time a few years back when I may have been considered for the job. There was an opening for the player personnel director before Rick was hired, and I thought that maybe I might have been in consideration for the job. Meanwhile, Rick had been let go in Miami and was looking for work. Rob had known Rick in Miami and I had known him for many years when he was with the Detroit Lions, Chicago Bears, and then Miami before being considered for the Vikings job. He had paid his dues and was a very good friend of mine.

I'll never forget the day I was cutting the grass in the backyard and I got a phone call from Zygi Wilf. He wanted to ask me about Rick. The conversation basically boiled down to, "You are asking me to promote a guy for a job that I was potentially interested in." But it was okay, it really was. I don't think I was really suited for the job anyway. It wasn't my cup of tea. It wasn't a job that fit my way of doing things, and Rick was a good friend.

I told Zygi, "I can't say anything bad about the guy. I know how hard he works and I would certainly endorse him for the job if I wasn't a candidate." I was fine with that, and was almost more relieved than I was disappointed. Rick was the right man for the job and I have been convinced for a long time that the team certainly made the right hire.

Trading is another effective way to gain the right personnel. When the team is going to make a trade for a player on another roster, our pro department is relied upon heavily. Their job is to look at the players on other teams and make evaluations on them. Most of the player trades are done outside the draft. The majority of these trades are made in training camp or during the season, up to trade deadline.

Ultimately you are looking to fill holes in your team. Maybe you wanted to fill a need in the draft but it didn't materialize, so you use the trade option to fill that particular need. Ryan Monnens is also a key person in that arena and he has really grown to be an important figure.

On the flip side, when a player is released, there is a whole chain of people in the organization involved. Rick, Rob, and Mike Zimmer, as well as many others, may all enter into the picture. It is not a pleasant experience to release or cut a player, but it is one of those things that has to be done.

It's a tough job to let someone know that you are letting him go, but it is also part of the game. Fortunately I never had to endure anything like that as a player. I consider myself lucky in that regard. These guys make a lot of good friends in the locker room, and a lot of them have permanently moved here, so it is a tough pill to swallow. I'm sure it's hard to say goodbye because they work hard and try to do their best. At the same time, you have to do what's best for your football team, so it comes with the territory.

I have said many times, I looked forward to going to work every day. It was special to me. As I look back on my life, I can't think of any wholesale changes I'd make other than I wish I'd tried a lot harder in school and gotten better grades, that type of thing. I really believe someone was watching over me. I was able to have a long career in a very tough industry. I feel very fortunate to have stayed healthy as a player and had the ability to transition into the scouting world with the same team for many years. It has been quite a journey.

When I think about being a scout, I was very lucky to have people like Frank Gilliam and Jerry Reichow guide me along the way. Conrad Cardano was a very good mentor as well. They all had different qualities about them, things I emulated.

Frank and Conrad were exceptional workers, and Jerry had a great feel for what he did. That's not to say he didn't work as hard, but he had a different personality. He was never too high and never too low. He was always very even-keeled. He didn't get rattled by things and he didn't get stressed. These guys all worked long hours and had a great feel for the game—and they also made it fun for everyone. You enjoyed being around them, but you still always knew that you had to get the work done while having a good time doing it. They were all exceptional at what they did and were exceptional individuals.

I would like to think I was a good player and a good scout. I might have championed the overachiever role to a certain extent, but I consider myself that. It was important to me. I wanted to make sure that I carried my share of the workload and maybe more. I was very loyal to the people I worked for and worked with. I feel like I had a good background for it and a good work ethic for it. I feel I had a good eye for it as well. I think, like anything else, you had to put in the time.

My family made a tremendous amount of sacrifices in order for me to be able to do my job. There were times when there was a lot of overkill on my part that took away from the time I could be at home. But it was the only way I knew how to do it. When you do something, you have to be 100 percent all in. I felt I needed to do it that way to be successful.

With Frank and Jerry in the organization they never were surprised by anything. They had seen it all and done it all. They were football guys, that's what they cared about. It's where their passion was and their entire focus was on winning championships. I have always felt that the amount of respect that you have for people—whether it's those you work with, work for, spend time with, those you consider friends, the people that you love—is what loyalty is all about. I learned that as a kid from my parents. They have been married for well over 60 years. To see the love and respect that they have for each other has impressed me greatly, and I think I learned about loyalty from them. I think you should model your life that way and live by that. And when you do, then you are going to get it back from other people.

The best part of being a scout for the Minnesota Vikings was that it afforded me the opportunity to stay in the business after I retired from playing football. It was really the focal point of my entire career. To be able to stay in a game that is so important to me and that I love so much meant more than I could ever explain. To be able to stay in an industry with a team that I was very comfortable with and had tremendous passion for was more than I could ever have asked for.

To remain with an organization that took a chance on me at the beginning, set me up for the rest of my working life, was truly an honor. It was a great fit and a wonderful gift for me and my family.

CHAPTER TEN

Colleges and Universities—Scouting's Bread and Butter

Over the course of a scouting year I probably went to 75 to 85 schools. There are certain programs, the upper echelon of the championship programs, I'd go to every year no matter what, and then there were the others. These were the smaller schools, which may have only one or two players that you will want to take a look at. It's the I-AA, Division II, and the Division III schools that you wouldn't go into every year. But every once in a while they would have a player or two who would come to our attention, and you would go and spend a full day there.

I went to all of the Big Ten schools, especially early in my career because that was my region of the country. They were, for the most part, extremely good visits. Some of the head coaches and schools were much looser than others, while some had a lot of restrictions on the scouts.

The Big Ten was great because you could drive and get to the next place easily, as opposed to conferences like the PAC-12 and the SEC, where the schools were so spread out. You could zip through Michigan and Ohio and Illinois and Indiana and Iowa and get a lot of the schools done rather quickly without spending so much time on the road in between. Minnesota and Wisconsin were close also. When you have schools that are fairly close together it takes considerably less time than getting on an airplane and flying all over the place.

Typically schools want you to call and let them know when you would like to come in and visit, so they knew who was going to be there on any given day. It was the courteous thing to do to show your respect for them and the fact that you were their guest. We would make the calls ourselves or someone in our office would set it up for us. They just needed a heads-up to know who was coming and for how long. Each school typically had someone who was a pro liaison, or an administrative assistant who would handle scheduling. Most of the time we would only spend a day at a school, but occasionally we might be there for a day and a half or even two. At some of the larger schools, where they may have 13, 14, or 15 prospects, you might spend a day and a half or more.

Some of these schools—the University of Michigan, for example— had numerous restrictions. Schools might allow you to come on only certain days or certain weeks. Often the access was limited. This was okay with me, because I knew what they expected. We could always work out our schedules accordingly. If all the schools operated that way, however, it would make it very hard for scouts to do their jobs.

Every year in training camp we would meet with Rick and go through a manual that he prepared for the scouts. We would get our schedules prepared during that week knowing that we would make adjustments along the way. At the end of the scouts' camp visit there would be a huge composite made of all the schedules, so that each scout knew where everyone else would be all the time. Again, there would be adjustments in the schedules as time went on, but we tried to stick with our predetermined schedules. It wasn't uncommon to overlap at a lot of schools because we would want some players to get more of a look—and with the restrictions, you might have two scouts at the same school at the same time. We had a very veteran staff who knew how to schedule, so it wasn't nearly as complicated as it sounds. Kelly Wilske and Kelly Kleine would do the organizing. Luckily, in today's computer-driven world, it is much easier than it used to be.

Once the schedule was in place, on any given day of the month I knew where all the scouts were going to be, though those appointments could change for a variety of reasons. Maybe one scout would see a guy and think that the player was good enough to get another look. If we graded him up he would always get some more looks and evaluations. We would alert the group if there were any major changes to the prospect list or any significant add-ons with daily and regular weekly updates.

Our contacts at the schools were typically coaches, though it could be someone else assigned to handle the scouting departments for the NFL teams. Every school was different. Our contact would be the point person for our daily schedule and for the player. They were the individual you would sit down with at the school to learn about the player. These point people were critical for our day at each school.

After the morning meetings and after we got our tape work done, we would typically have some time before practice in the afternoon. On those occasions, we might try to see the position coach or even the head coach if they were available. Even though I had a clear agenda as to what I needed to get done, there was usually time to get additional information if needed. Seeing the other coaches was very beneficial— especially if you could touch base with the head coach.

I would say that most of the schools were cooperative, but it was like anything else: You had to establish a certain level of trust or demonstrate your track record first. Once you did that, it would go a long way.

Scouts have to remember when you go into these schools that you are their guest, and whatever information that you get from the schools is complimentary information that is not required or mandated. They have to understand that they have a job to do, but that the people they are getting the information from are first and foremost employees of their own program, not the NFL. They are not obligated to share any, much less all, of their information. I always tried to be very courteous and give great respect to everyone who I came in contact with when I went into schools. Without those schools and our contacts, it would be so much harder to do the job. Getting along and respecting the protocol was of the utmost importance.

After practices were over for the day, we were essentially done— except for one thing, which has changed completely over the years. When the coaches arrange for practice in the morning, it puts the entire day on a different schedule. But that's okay, because the scouts have to adjust. If we want the information we need, we need to be nimble to work around their schedules. The early practice schedule gets the players up and moving early, so they have to schedule their classes later on in the day. A lot of the coaches prefer that kind of a schedule.

You might be at practice for 20 minutes or you might be there for an hour and a half. It depends on the school, the program, and their schedule. At Alabama, you could sit there and watch their practice all day if you wanted to do that—and for a program as successful as theirs, they were exceptional in that regard.

It all changes from year to year and from day to day. Typically a 2:30 to 3:00 PM practice was the best because it gave you plenty of time to get your work done and get a start on your reports. I usually stayed for a portion of practice to eyeball the prospects and get a feel for their agility. You could see how the players moved around in agility drills and those types of things. And when the prospects know that there are pro scouts around, believe me, they are on their toes to create positive impressions. Then, if there was time, it was off to the next school.

The majority of these schools would want you to leave when they start working on their game plans for their upcoming opponents, and it's kind of an unwritten rule that at that time, maybe it's time for the scouts to head out.

Some of the small schools that had smaller groups of prospects could easily be handled on a single day, and you could get all your work done early. That wasn't possible with some of the major schools and programs. At some schools, you might be in a room with multiple scouts on any given day, particularly if they had restrictions on scout visits. Some of the schools might open for scouts only on Tuesday or Wednesday; others only in the month of October. We had to be very flexible in our schedules and open to changes, but we always got the job done.

Watching the film of the players gave us a good handle on guys' playing ability, but there was still so much more that you wanted to know. It was all about getting background information. *What makes these guys tick?* You formulate your opinion on the player's ability from the tape. And then you fill it in with intangibles. *Are there any flaws in his personality? How does he learn the game? Has he had issues off the field? How does he work out in the weight room? Does he get along well with his teammates? Is he coachable? Is he football smart but maybe not book smart?*

You have to dot all the I's and cross all the T's when it comes to the player's character. You would want to know about the player's family situation. *How were they raised or what kind of background do they come from?* For some of these players, going from where they came from to where they are in college is remarkable. Some come from very tough backgrounds and have endured tough upbringings. They're survivors, and that is a real tribute to their character and their resiliency. Guys like that, with the mental toughness to overcome adversity, scored big in my book.

Some schools may try to oversell their players; others are very transparent. Some will tell us what they think of the players rather than what we need to hear, but the reality is that it is good for the schools when they get their players drafted or signed. It helps them with recruiting, ticket sales, their success rate, and job security.

For the most part though, I have always felt that the majority of schools are pretty honest in their assessments and the information that they are willing to share with us. There are a lot of people who you can talk to at most programs, so you can get a variety of opinions. But in the end, the only one that really matters is the one that you develop about that player. How you feel about the player is the key.

We usually get the real scoop on a player, especially if he is a real jerk off the field. But ultimately what we want to know is whether that player will be able to succeed at the NFL level. *Will he be able to handle the stress of making the team? How will he fit in? Does he adjust well to difficult situations?* These are all things that are important to know.

I had a few favorite schools that I really enjoyed going to scout. I attended the University of Illinois, so I enjoyed going back there. Iowa was always a great school to visit too. Coach Ferentz is an outstanding football coach, and you always knew what you were going to get when you went in there. Ohio State was always a good visit. Wisconsin has always been a very good visit—for all of the scouts, not just us. And P.J. Fleck at Minnesota has been very good at letting us in. In the SEC, Alabama was outstanding. Miami and Florida State were good too, as were the rest of the schools in that conference.

The bigger, more successful programs are more regimented because they might have multiple scouts there all the time when the program is open. By contrast, a school like Bemidji State may have just a handful of scouts come in all season.

Some of these programs will have coaching changes—that's inevitable if you stay in scouting for a long time. The number of changes that makes in your routine varies; some have minor changes to their programs and some are very different. Again, we learn to adjust.

As far as the head coaches go, they are all very different. Some are very accessible and you can get information directly from them; others are off-limits completely, or too busy with all their daily business to visit with us. I mean, these are very busy people, putting in game plans, looking over their offense or defense...all the duties and chores of a head football coach. It's understandable.

Which is why I was always so grateful to get a head coach's ear. When Pete Carroll was at the University of Southern California, I would always be able to find him at some point during the day—he would carve out some time for me. Pete was just great about that. He would invariably give me time to talk about their prospects in spite of his busy day.

Other head coaches would stick their heads in the scouting room and give us their insight on particular players. I always appreciated that when they came into a room and said hi to the scouts and asked them if they had any questions. Others I found to be very aloof and wouldn't give you the time of day, and that's okay too.

There were a few schools that were very problematic. That was usually a reflection of the head coach; they were paranoid about letting the scouts in and giving the scouts information. Maybe they had a bad experience with certain scouts; that happens. Not everybody plays by the rules, and if that's the case, then shame on the scout. For the most part, I found most schools to be very cooperative. They made your day easy to manage.

When you are out on visits, you are always looking for that piece of information that no one else has. But for the most part, everybody has access to the same information on players, so it comes down to how you interpret it. It's how you evaluate a player on tape, and how you evaluate the player during practice or in a game. That kind of information becomes pretty subjective. There are always little bits of information about a given player that everyone tries to get a leg up on. But the basic foundation of each player's background is pretty universal. Every scout gets access basically to the same information. Sure, there is always going to be a scout who has a relationship with a coach at a certain school, and maybe he will get a piece of information that he decides not to share, but for the most part it is shared.

It was a high priority for me to treat others the same way that I would like to be treated if I was in their position. As I have said before and I want to repeat it because it is so important: the scout is a guest at the school. You come and go when they ask you to come and go. You show up on time and you don't interfere. You never overstep your boundaries and you respect the rules and the program.

The reputation that I had playing 14 years in the NFL helped me somewhat. I think that any scout, if he was lucky enough to have played professionally, would have the respect of the schools and coaches. A playing career doesn't make you smarter than anyone else or better than anyone else, but maybe it gives you a little edge because schools and players know you have been through that grind and that you understand what it is all about. They know that you know how hard it is to play at any level, so you get respect for what you have done. Of course, you still have to earn it with your actions; they won't just give it to you.

It was important to communicate with our other Vikings scouts, especially with cross-checks. Good factual communication is always valuable, just as in any other kind of business. It was vitally important that we passed on information to other scouts before they made their visits. Maybe the player had been injured for a few weeks and had taken a while to come back, for example. If he was injured, how long did it take him to get healthy? Or is he playing hurt? This is all good information and important to share.

You may go into a school right after a loss and everybody is tight-lipped and buttoned up, which can make getting information harder. If they are not having a successful season, that may cause problems too. Any given day is different. The bigger schools obviously require more work than the smaller schools, but the people are generally the same and will help you get your work done.

A lot of schools enjoy having the scouts in there because it is good for their program. And as I said before, the players know and may work just a touch harder if they know an NFL scout is watching them. Scouts have a very important role in deciding who will get drafted. Players know this, so it is just natural for them to give their very best.

You would like to see that in a player every day, but that is not reality for most players.

When we went back to our hotel to do the reports, we had a format that we followed. The reports included the player's height and weight and specific boxes for other traits about him. We would give a numeric grade to his height, weight, speed, agility, arm length, and durability. Then there are position specifics, along with an injury box for those specifics. You recorded on the form the games that you watched on film, along with the positives and negatives.

Basically, I recorded all the factual information that I obtained on the player, and everything subjectively that I learned. The summary of the report is really important because it tells what you know about the player other than his physical attributes. That's where you see how they might fit or factor in as a player and more specifically with the Minnesota Vikings. Is this guy going to fit with our depth and roster during this particular year, and is he going to be able to come in and upgrade us? Or maybe he won't impact our roster this year but has a chance to make the team as a practice squad player. Or maybe he is more of a developmental player, so you grade him accordingly. All the forms and formats for all the teams are more or less the same.

When I decided to retire from scouting, I knew somewhat ahead of time, so when I went into the schools I was able to say my goodbyes for the most part. I hadn't decided exactly when, but I was able to tell the friends I had made over the years. And you can only imagine how many relationships that I had made during 28 years of scouting.

Leaving the Vikings organization was the toughest part, because the one thing you will always miss, whether it be in football or anything else, is the people.

CHAPTER ELEVEN

Game Ready

There is definitely a different type of preparation for high school football and college football players than there is for pros. With high schoolers, time is so limited. You are in school all day, have very short meetings with the coaches, and then you go out and practice. There is not nearly as much exposure to the game.

There is a small amount of carryover from high school to college, but the leap from college to pro is very different. It is much more intensified, the meeting times are much more frequent. And in professional football, the coaches have a captive audience. This is a player's full-time job.

I started lifting weights when I was in high school. I understood that I had to get bigger if I wanted to play football down the road. I mentioned that I was only five foot two and weighed 110 pounds as a freshman, so at the time my future was not very bright. I grew a foot and gained about 100 to 110 pounds in high school.

I got interested in lifting weights when I started to grow, so this was very beneficial to me at every level of play. In the late 1960s and even in the early 1970s, there was not a lot of interest in weight training. Some athletes may have done it because they played a sport, but usually they did what was asked of them and it would end there. But I was on a never-ending mission to keep myself in top physical shape, and my size and gains in strength became visible, so I had something to show for it. I went to a gym called the Pit. It was there for a lot of the athletes around the Evansville area and is still open today. They even had a competitive lifting team there as well.

The pressure and time commitment of meetings and workout times rapidly increased when I got to the collegiate level. The increase in time and preparation was night and day compared to high school. In college you are basically "getting paid" by being on scholarship, so it's almost like a job. The game gradually gets more intense and competitive as you move from high school to college to professional football.

Once I moved into the professional level it was very different from the beginning to the end. Under Bud, the player's days wouldn't start until late in the morning, and we would be out of there generally by 5:00. By the end of my career, the workload was much heavier. We would be there all day.

Today's players are there for meetings and practice, but many also spend a lot of time on their own studying film, working out, and otherwise preparing themselves for the upcoming game. It's a job, and it's big business. Players have to find some kind of edge to be successful.

When I got drafted by Minnesota, we went to training camp at Mankato for seven weeks, and there were six preseason games. Think about that: we had six preseason games. In 2020, because of

COVID-19, we had *no* preseason, so the evaluation of players was significantly diminished from 1977 to 2020.

As I mentioned, when I got drafted, I got a call from Patty Crowe, who was the administrative assistant to the player personnel staff. She told me, "You were drafted by the Minnesota Vikings in the ninth round and we will see you in August." That was it. There wasn't a lot of big money back then—maybe a few guys who were making upwards of $100,000, but that was about it. I have no idea what the coaches were making, but the increase in salaries in today's game is dramatic.

Before my first training camp, I dedicated the entire summer to getting myself ready for football. I wanted to make the team and I was going to be ready. I worked out the entire summer. I would have conditioning days when I would run distance or run long sprints, run intervals, and then lift with my legs one day and upper body the next. I was basically training every day to get ready for camp in the summer of 1977.

Overall, most of our training was done separate from the team. We didn't have a training facility until they built Winter Park, so I was a member at Life Time Fitness and did my training there as we got closer to camp as well as once the season began. The Vikings did not do a lot of conditioning under Bud.

In training camp we practiced twice a day. I think Bud saw training camp as a way to get the players in shape, but there was still an expectation that you would come to camp well-conditioned. If players wanted to lift weights or do other conditioning, they had to figure out a way to do it on their own.

Bud had us do some things in camp to get in shape. We would do up-and-downs (burpees) just about every practice. We would do a lot of stretching and some conditioning work, but not a lot. Bud never worked us too hard. He never wanted us to be overtired or wear us out before the season began.

We were in pads twice a day, doing drills and scrimmaging. So just that in and of itself got us into pretty good playing shape. Indeed, by the time we got done with training camp we were in playing shape and ready to go. Bud had a very precise reason for everything he did, and it proved successful for him.

I can't recall what the exact cut dates were for players, but it was similar to today. The roster was finalized before the last preseason game. Bud never did a lot of shuffling with the roster since he was content with the players that he had, so there was not a lot of turnover early in my career.

We had a veteran football team; Bud knew it and kept it that way. The team had been together for a long time. When our class got there, five rookies made the team that year, and I believe that was probably the most that had made it for quite some time.

I worried a little about getting cut that first year, but after the first week or so I felt I could match up with the competition. I felt that I could compete at that level, not only with the players on offense but with those at my position as well. I was as big and strong as most of them, with the exception of Matt Blair, who had unusual size and athleticism for a linebacker.

The game was not as complicated as it is today in its learning, formation, and motion. People basically just lined up and ran the football. There were minimal formation changes and personnel packages. That kind of played into my hand from a coverage perspective. We didn't have all of the defensive combinations that they have today, much less any of the exotic ones. We had 11 starters on defense and we were basically on the field for most of the game.

I was very impressed by the previous success of the team when I arrived in training camp. This was a very good football team. I'll repeat myself a little bit here because I love to say it. My first year we went to the NFC Championship Game. The Vikings had gone to the Super Bowl three out of the four previous years. I mean, I was starting to think that this was a routine thing for Minnesota: we would go to (at least) the championship game every year, and the Super Bowl three out of four years. I really thought it was going to continue. Well, it didn't.

I think most of the players had the same expectations. The other teams in the division were struggling. But our team was getting older, and it ended up being 10 years before we made it back to the conference championship game.

We made a little extra money in my first year when we went to the NFC championship, and again, I expected it to be an ongoing thing for a long time. It's very hard to win it all, as the Vikings well know after four Super Bowl losses, but it was quite a run that we had and it probably spoiled several of the new players for quite a while.

The young players in particular came to find out exactly how difficult it was to win on a regular basis, let alone make it all the way to the Super Bowl. Think how many great teams the Vikings have had over the years. We haven't been back to the Super Bowl in what seems like a lifetime.

When I got there many of the players had other things going on off the field. Some had jobs outside of football, some had other interests. When the season ended, there were many players you didn't see again until training camp the following season. Some lived in and around the Twin Cities, but others lived out of state. Everyone ran in their own different circles, and that became increasingly common as the years went by.

Tommy Kramer and I were roommates for more than six years—until we each got engaged and married in 1983 and 1984, respectively. Tommy and I remained roommates in camp and on the road, and he is still a very good friend. I still see him from time to time and it is always good to catch up with him. We have gone in different directions and have had different careers after playing, but will always remember the time we had together. Times change and we change and go our separate ways. But I will always cherish his friendship.

The preseason was different once you established yourself as a starter because you knew you were only going to be in the game for a quarter or half. It was important to fine-tune things and get prepared for the season.

As soon as the last preseason game was over, everything ramped up because we knew that we were now playing for keeps. Everything got more serious. Every game counted. There was pressure on everybody as we moved forward.

The three head coaches during my career were Bud, Les Steckel, and Jerry Burns. They were all different in their approaches to the game and how the follow-up after a game worked.

Every week during the regular season was basically the same. We would come in on Monday and go through the film. We would also go out for a short workout just to be sure the bumps and bruises were not too severe. Tuesday was an off day, but a lot of players would come around to lift weights, get treatment, or watch tape of our upcoming opponent. The community Tuesdays started after my career was over.

Today's Vikings go out into the community to hospitals, schools, and a variety of other places where they can make a difference and give back.

Back then most of the guys that did work out in the community did it in the off-season. The community Tuesdays that we have today was mostly started when Denny Green became the head coach. It was after my playing days.

I didn't start on a regular basis until my third year with the team, though, as I mentioned earlier, I did start three games my rookie season because Jeff Siemon was hurt. I was a regular on all of our special teams. We had Matt Blair, Wally Hilgenberg, and Fred McNeil as linebackers, and they each had great careers with the Vikings.

Once Winter Park was built I generally went to the office and would do a workout on Tuesdays, in addition to preparing for the game and our opponent for that week. On Wednesdays, we were basically there the entire day as the years went by (as opposed to Bud's four- to five-hour day).

As the years went on it became a necessary thing for all the players to put in the time. We had meetings early in the morning, lunch, and then went out to practice to work on the game plan. Today, the players might have lunch and dinner at the facility. It has become an 8- to 10-hour day for the players, and their schedule changes with Monday and Thursday night games, creating long or short weeks.

When I came into the league the offenses were not as creative as today. Most teams ran with basically the same personnel throughout the whole game, and they didn't have all the matchup groups and exotic formations. We didn't see three receiver sets very often. People liked running the football, as opposed to taking the high-percentage pass in today's game. You might see some two–tight end or three-wide schemes, but the game has become much more complex and intricate.

Defensively, in my day we might have had a few man and zone coverages and a few blitz packages, but that was it—nothing like what's in use in today's game. The game has become a lot more specialized and complicated, which in turn requires more time to prepare. Recognition, personnel, movement, motion, and snap counts…it has all changed.

I think the changes are good for the game. It has evolved, and the coaches are more creative. It is a matchup game now. *How can you create the best matchups to be sure that you are on the winning side at the end of the day?* Coaches try to match up their best players with the other team's weak spots. It is a chess match more than it is just lining up and beating people because you are better than them physically. There is constant strategy from the beginning to the end of a game.

Under Bud, after the game was over he never wanted any contact with the opposing team. He never had any contact with the opposing coach, never shook hands or anything like that. That's the way he was. It was kind of an unwritten rule of Bud's to get off the field. That was his personality, and he didn't want you fraternizing with the other team either. You knew that's the way he was. He didn't have to tell you. He didn't have to remind you. You just knew. It was expected. It was all business, and that was fine with me. That's the way it was.

That philosophy kind of trickled down to Les and Jerry. They weren't quite the sticklers that Bud was, but close. It certainly is much different today. Whether it is right, wrong, or indifferent, I kind of believe in Bud's philosophy. I mean, you are going into battle for three and a half hours. You really don't want to go and shake hands with your opponents after the game! At least that's the way I looked at it.

I know I was pretty intense on game day—at least I hope I was. That's what you work on all week, to be intense and to play well. You work all week for those three and a half hours on Sunday. The expected outcome is to win the football game. That's the ultimate goal, and it doesn't matter if you played well and didn't win the game. Winning is everything in this league. So with that in mind, you do everything in your power to win the football game. And if you don't get it done, it's almost like a week's worth of work went down the drain.

The way I approached the game was to look at all of the week's work that I did in preparation for the game and to view that as important as anything else—certainly as important as getting in the right frame of mind before the game. If I knew that I had prepared well in advance of the game, getting myself game ready would not be as difficult. I think if you are prepared physically and mentally and you feel good about the game plan, you are in good shape for the game.

I needed to know what our opposition was going to do in *this* situation and what they were going to do in *that* situation and what they were going to do with their formations. All of that kind of preparation has to be done during the week through the film study of the opponent's offense. If you do it right and if you feel good about it, then the odds are in your favor that you are going to have success on game day.

My demeanor before a game was very focused. We all had our individual rituals. I would get taped by the same trainer. Toward the end of my career I would always go out and play catch with Pete Carroll, who was our defensive backs coach at the time. (I know that relationship helped when I was a scout and Pete was at USC.)

I prepared routinely but I wouldn't necessarily call myself superstitious. I never had to always put my socks on a certain way or anything like that. I just prepared the same way before each game. I would go out and stretch and loosen up to get ready. It was important to me to be sure that I had dotted all the I's and crossed all the T's when I did my job on the field calling the defensive alignment, making sure we were all on the same page.

We had to be sure that we were doing things right both mentally and physically. For the three and a half hours that we were out there, I felt that I was pretty focused on the game and the game plan. Game day was very intense, and it took a while to wind down after the game. We got there early, leaving enough time to get ourselves ready to go and play a football game. For me, it got easier rather than harder as time went by because I felt certain I had done what I needed to do to get myself ready to play.

There were always a few things that would change on game day when the offense would put in a little different wrinkle and you had to adjust to it. I think that was part of the fun of the giant chess match, along with trying to be more physical than the guy across from you.

I have been asked many times about what Bud would say in the locker room before a game. I would say this: none of them—Bud, Steckel, or Burns—was very demonstrative. They were not Lombardi or Rockne, that's for sure. They all had their own unique style. Bud was very straightforward. That was his personality. He was calm and to the point, and he told you what he expected from us collectively. It was a very matter-of-fact talk: "Let's go out and do our job and see how the chips fall." Les was more fiery. He was younger and more hyper. Burnsie was very colorful—more on the X-rated side than the PG side.

After a game you could always tell if they were upset by the way we played, and justifiably so. They had all been around long enough that they understood players should be ready to play without a rousing pregame speech to get going. It was obvious they all felt that we should be ready to play individually and collectively as a team. Anything they could do to change the outcome of the game through a speech was not in the cards. The coaches put us in a position to make plays; if we did not do it, then it was on us players.

It was pretty much the same routine when we went on the road. We did all the same things, except we were away from home. There were not any significant changes that the coaches made. One thing: they would always reflect on the fact that you have to beat the team, but you also have to beat the crowd. Our preparation was the same. It was a business trip, and our goal was to go out and win a football game. The job was very simple: take the team and their hometown crowd out of the game.

Our coaches always talked after the game, win or lose. The difference between winning and losing is paramount. The swing between winning and losing is so dramatic that it is actually hard to explain. I guess I would say that you feel terrible when you lose and are absolutely ecstatic when you win. The gamut of emotions that you face is unbelievable, and everyone reacts differently. Some guys take longer than others to get over it. It is a huge team game, and when you win, some of your play can be overlooked. On the other hand, when you lose, everything is up for grabs and dissected.

After a game, Jenny and I would typically go out to eat with her family or some teammates, maybe have a couple of beers—anything to kind of relax and settle down. It probably took me a good couple of days, maybe until Tuesday, before I was really somewhat back to normal—and that's win or lose. Of course, it is easier to digest the wins than the losses. After the losses you are always going to second-guess what you could have done more of, or what you could have done less of. *Did we do too much? Did we not do enough in preparation?* I always felt like my effort was there, but when you have a bad day you hope it's not on a Sunday.

When I talk about effort, I mean both myself and the team. I tried to be consistent all of the time. And I think for the most part our teams were always pretty consistent. In any given game, there are probably five or six plays that determine the outcome. Some days you are just off and some days you are really on. It's the teams that don't have the off days that always seem to find a way to win. The teams that can produce at a high level week in and week out are the teams that are going to be successful.

Some players make a tremendous difference as individuals, especially quarterbacks. Take the New England Patriots. In 2020, without Tom Brady, they struggled. I mean, Brady is a first-ballot Hall of Famer. And of course we know what happened with Brady in Tampa Bay. They won the Super Bowl. You just cannot say enough for the quarterback position. Green Bay with Bart Starr, Brett Favre, and Aaron Rodgers have had consistency at quarterback for more than 40 years. These kinds of franchise players don't come along that often. Guys like Brady and Drew Brees of New Orleans are very unique, and they can make a tremendous difference.

Once you get a franchise quarterback, you have to keep him, period. The stability at that position is critical. The Vikings had Tarkenton and Kramer for a long time, and Daunte Culpepper had tremendous

tools, potential, and production before he got hurt. It is really important to try to get one of these franchise quarterbacks. Sometimes it's
pure luck, and other times the person just develops, but when you try
to draft one and he doesn't work out, it can really set the team back, in
some cases for many years.

When I was playing and things went bad right from the beginning
of the game, the most important thing was to try to just settle down
and not start pressing. Whether it is you individually or collectively as
a team, you try to get things back on track. All it takes sometimes is
one or two plays to get back in the game. Sometimes those plays never
happen and you struggle all day. But you have to play disciplined and
play within the scheme, because if you lose that, then things will really
go bad for you no matter what. When players lose discipline, lack
attention to detail, get their alignments wrong, and start freelancing,
then you are in big trouble.

I used to get upset with people on the other side of the ball from
time to time. We played against our divisional rivals twice a year and
you got to know the players on those teams pretty well. You got to
know them on and off the field and of course everyone had a job to
do, but sometimes some players did a little extra that would aggravate
me. There is no room in football for some of their play. There were
certain teams that generated an extra incentive for their players, especially the NFC Central teams like Green Bay, Chicago, and Detroit.
Those games were always a dogfight. And generally at some point in
the schedule the division championship would be on the line.

I was never a big talker like a Johnny Randle. He was unbelievable as a talker; he really knew how to get the other team's goat.
I kept quiet and tried to encourage my teammates as opposed to

bantering with my opponent. On occasion I would get upset at a teammate—although it really wasn't anger in that sense but more disappointment. And I tried to convey encouragement to them rather than disappointment, although perhaps it didn't always come off that way.

I understand that everybody makes mistakes and I certainly had my share, but that's a part of the game. No one plays a perfect game. We're humans. You have to take that into account and understand it. You have to be flexible in the way you judge people. At the end of the day that's not your job, it's the coaches' job.

When the season ended, it took some time to decompress. I would take a few days off and then I would go to a health club and begin my workouts again. I would get on the treadmill or get on the bike or start lifting weights. For me it was a year-round job.

The off-season was a time for taking care of nagging injuries and letting your mind and body heal. During the season, there is no time for any of that. You had to be ready to go again in a matter of just a few days. You also had to reflect back on the season: how you performed as an individual, how you performed as a defense, how you performed as a team. As you evaluated all of this you had to be self-critical. You had to determine what you could do as an individual to make the next year a better year.

But the off-season was family time, a time to reset. Without the stress and the strain of being in-season, we all had a lot of free time to spend with our wives and kids, and that was great.

I also hung around with several of the players during the off-season. I had some friends that I would golf and play racquetball with. And once we finally built a facility at Winter Park, I would see many of my teammates more often. We had racquetball courts and two weight rooms and an indoor bubble, so we got together and worked out more frequently. And then the Vikings built their indoor practice fields—that was really great. Over time, the off-season became a lot more regimented, and you would go and train with your teammates who were in town. Still, it's different from today, when off-season programs are mandatory.

Some of the teammates that I spent time with were Tommy Kramer, Rickey Young, Mark Mullaney, Keith Millard, Bob Bruer, Jim Hough, Keith Nord—all those people were at the facility a lot. The guys that lived in town were typically the ones that spent the most time at the facility.

I always felt like we had a very good chemistry in the locker room; guys always got along with each other. It was a fairly close-knit group of guys year to year, and everyone had everyone else's best interests in mind. It was great to be a part of that kind of an atmosphere. We did a good job of managing all of the personalities.

We had some contact with the coaches during the off-season, but for the most part our livelihood was down on the lower level of the facility and their livelihood was upstairs. Our interaction with the coaches was always good. I felt like we had good communication with them. And I always felt that we could learn something from the coaches, both on and off the field. The working relationships that we had were helpful and encouraging.

The linebackers coaches who worked with me were good men and great teachers. Jocko Nelson, Maxie Baughan, Floyd Reese, and Monte Kiffin—all of them were great guys and exceptional coaches. I had some excellent position coaches over the course of my career.

I started out playing at the old Metropolitan Stadium. One of the places we practiced at was Midway Stadium in St. Paul, and then when the Twins were done for the year we would move into the old Met for the majority of the time. The reality was we would practice all over the place. We practiced at the old Minneapolis Armory, in a park by Lake Nokomis, at the University of Minnesota, and other places where we could get the space.

I loved playing at the old Met Stadium. It was probably not a great place to watch a game from a fan's perspective, but it was a great place to play. We had the 12th Man in the weather at times; many of the teams from warmer climates hated coming here, which was something that Bud really thrived on. It was just a great atmosphere. Fans would come early and stay late. I thought it was just a tremendous setting in which to play football.

Early in my career at the old Metropolitan Stadium we had a lot of fan interaction. Fans hung around where the players parked their cars, so we had wonderful interactions with them after the game. We would even sometimes go out after the game and have a couple beers with the fans. I know we lost some of the intimacy when we moved indoors to the Metrodome. It was a special time we had with the Met—the fans, the weather, and the games—and I believe that setting had a lot to do with our success. It was a time when the fans were close to us physically and could share the game with us. I enjoyed it—I really did.

Once we moved inside to the Metrodome, we basically lost that advantage. Though the noise and volume at the Metrodome were just fantastic. It became absolutely deafening at times. We lost the weather advantage, but gained something from crowd noise. It was a good place to play football from a fan's perspective. Now there's U.S. Bank Stadium—what an unbelievable building and tremendous venue in which to watch a Vikings game!

As I said before, as a young player I enjoyed playing at the old Met. It was rough-and-ready. By the end of the year there was no grass left due to the cold weather, so they were basically spray-painting the field green. The field conditions were not ideal, and the elements made it difficult, but when you are 22, 23, or 24 years old? Hell, you could go and play in the parking lot and it wouldn't matter.

I enjoyed the Metrodome. We had a lot of success in there—and a lot of disappointment as well. It was home for us, and always you knew what the weather conditions were going to be inside! I felt we had home-field advantage at both places but preferred the old Metropolitan Stadium. I could have played there my entire career.

I think Bud and I shared the same thoughts about going to play inside. He was likely not a huge fan of the whole idea. I think he liked the advantages we had late in the fall. I think he liked to see the opposing teams struggle to stay warm when we were outside. I remember when we had that bubble at Winter Park. There would be six inches of snow on the ground and we would be out practicing right next to the bubble but we would not go in! Players complained loudly so that Bud would overhear them, but he wouldn't even acknowledge them. That was Bud. I'm not sure if he didn't want to go in there or if he wanted to show everyone who was in charge. I was never sure of the reason.

Green Bay was always a fun place to play on the road. It was kind of like playing at the old Met Stadium. When I first got here the Packers had split their home games between Green Bay and Milwaukee, and I liked playing in both places.

All in all, the most fun place to play was in Chicago against the Chicago Bears. Of course, I played for the University of Illinois, so Chicago was sort of like going home. Our rivalry was intense and we played at Soldier Field, which was a great place to play. In the mid-1980s, the Bears had become a very good football team. Going against Walter Payton and Jim McMahon was always a challenge for us. They had a great defense and a potent offense. It was the top of our rivalry games and always a tough one to play. The games were always so competitive and we got to know a lot of the Bears players. When we played them twice a year, we got to know some of their fans as well.

Detroit was a good place to play because we had a lot of success there (except when Barry Sanders was there). It was kind of like playing at the Metrodome, with the dome and all that came with it. I don't think the rivalry ever became comparable with playing the Bears and the Packers, though. It never caught fire like the other teams in our division. Probably because we had a lot of success there.

San Francisco was always a challenge to play on the road, as was Philadelphia. They both had good football teams and they both played outdoors. It was hard for us to play in some of the warmer places.

We didn't have to play some of the teams in the league on a regular basis. It was business as usual, but there wasn't that extra edge in playing them. Dallas was a tough place to play and win. They had a lot of good football teams, and we never had a lot of success down there. The Giants were another team that we enjoyed playing, even though we didn't play them very often.

I found that the fans were very special over the years. Giving autographs kind of goes with the territory. I have always appreciated their support. I appreciate them being very loyal fans to the Vikings and to me.

I feel like I have always been very receptive to fans' attention and I have always tried to give them the time that they deserve. Every once in a while it can be a little awkward, but most of the time fans are great. To this day I still get autograph requests on football cards. I read them all and send them back free of charge. It goes with the territory, and I feel that everyone should treat fans that way.

Occasionally someone will come up when we are out to dinner and want to have something signed or get an autograph. I don't have any issue with it and my wife doesn't have any issue with it, so it's fine. It's kind of the way it is, and I'm appreciative of them remembering me. Giving out an autograph after all these years is special for me. The majority of people who do approach are fans. I believe that the Minnesota Vikings have the best fans in the world, and I appreciate every last one of them. They are a big part of the game and will always be important to me.

CHAPTER TWELVE

Outside the Lines

I was thinking about Bud Grant and the way he carried himself, and a memory came to me. It was about three to four weeks into my rookie season, in training camp at Mankato, when it happened. Camp had been a grind and I had not talked to Bud at all—I mean, not a word. There had been no conversations, no sit-downs, no get-to-know-you gestures, nothing at all. He was pretty aloof, especially with the rookies.

We were in an afternoon practice, on the middle field at the south end. Bud used to run the scout team at practice, and for some reason I was standing next to him. Suddenly a butterfly flew over our heads and Bud started talking about the migration of the monarch butterfly. It was an unusual moment, odd for sure. He was not a man of a lot of words. I didn't know if he was probing to see what I knew about it or what he was doing, but I got a good lesson on the migration of the monarch butterfly nevertheless.

I didn't know what to think. *Why in the hell would our head football coach bring this up at practice?* I wondered. I didn't get it. He had not spoken a word to me before this one-sided conversation, and it set me back a little bit because it made no sense to me. I don't believe I said a word in response. I mean what could I have said? "Yes, Bud, they migrate very well." I don't think so. I was left speechless.

I never knew what kind of degree Bud earned in college but I wouldn't be surprised if it was psychology. He understood people. He knew how to control people's emotions and temperaments. He just knew exactly what to say at the right time to keep his troops in line.

Bud would sometimes bring his dog to practice on Saturday mornings because fall was hunting season. Wally Hilgenberg would also bring his dog, and it was so well trained it would sit at his locker for a couple hours. It was a different time in a different era; everything was a little more relaxed than it is today.

Jerry Burns was the character of all characters. Everyone on the team had a "middle name" with Burnsie and that was "Big Nuts." He would get so excited and carried away that when he talked on the practice field, in meetings, or face-to-face, he would forget your name. He would stutter and stammer and eventually he would call you Big Nuts. It was hilarious. You knew he knew your name, but he just got so worked up and carried away that he lost it—so Big Nuts it was. It was a term of endearment from Burnsie. He was so colorful. We would sit across from the offense with a partition dividing the meeting rooms and you could hear Burnsie over there yelling at the offense. It was comical. They would be laughing and then we would start laughing right along with them. He was one of the true characters in our business, that's for sure.

I mean absolutely no disrespect toward Burnsie. I loved the man and he was a great football coach, no question about that. Bill Walsh, the former San Francisco 49ers coach, got a lot of credit for the West Coast offense in pro football, but Burnsie ran that offense at Iowa and Minnesota long before Walsh emerged. He had that flair and ingenuity about him, and the ball-control offense was all Jerry Burns.

He was very intelligent, very funny, and a great communicator. He was good schematically and an excellent teacher of the game. He was a great coach and mentor. Some people will remember the character rather than the coach, but the bottom line was that he was very good at his job.

I don't know why Bud and Jerry got along so well because they were surely different personalities. I think there was a level of trust that they had gained over the years from being together and working together. Even when Bud was coaching in Canada he would have Jerry come up as a consultant and assist with their offense.

I'm sure Jerry was taken aback or even hurt when he didn't get the head coaching job after Bud retired the first time. Being a player, you are not really privy to any information around that decision—we had to just roll with the punches—but I would guess he was hurt. We players certainly were not consulted on who should get the job.

Despite the way things unfolded, he turned around and came back the next year and did a great job as offensive coordinator under Les Steckel, and eventually became our head coach. I had heard a lot of stories about the whole thing, but I am personally glad that he stayed because it paid off for both him and for us.

Burnsie was a great guy to work for, even as a defensive player. Being a captain and one of the older players on the team, we had a level of trust between us that is probably hard to find in today's game. I could go and sit down in his office, or he would pull me aside and we could talk about anything. He was one of those guys who players loved playing for and for whom we wanted to be successful.

After I retired, I would see Bud quite a bit. Bud kept an office at the team headquarters at Winter Park and has one now at the new facility. Once Burnsie left the coaching side he didn't come around much, except for alumni events or special occasions. I haven't seen much of Jerry the last couple of years, and I know he has had a tough go of it physically, but I know this: his sense of humor is still as sharp as ever. I mean, every time I see him—or Rickey Young, a former player—I just start laughing. They are both the kind of guys who always have something to say with kind of an edge to it. They just make me laugh. I don't think that Jerry ever got the credit that he deserves as a head coach. I always wished that we could have won a championship for Burnsie—and for Bud as well.

I played eight years for Bud, one with Les Steckel, and five with Jerry Burns. The year with Steckel was very difficult, as I mentioned previously. It was a very unusual year and anyone who was on the team that year will never forget it. That year with Les was a tough year for everybody. Not only did we lose Bud, who was the face of the franchise and the program, but along the way with Les, the season was miserable. He almost beat us into submission. By the third or fourth game of the season, we were almost finished, completely worn out both mentally and physically.

Just another quick note here on Steckel. As I have said, I liked Les and I got along with him, but his way of doing things was so different from the way we were used to, it made it hard to buy in. He was enthusiastic and energetic and I wanted him to succeed. I don't think there was anyone on the team that didn't want that. But as I said, he made it very hard for everyone. He changed too much and tried too hard to put his stamp on the program, and it didn't work out. It was a grueling off-season and training camp and there was live contact almost every day. The first few weeks of the season we were competitive but then it went downhill from there.

I mentioned Rickey Young as being a real character. Rickey was just one of those colorful guys. He had a smile on his face all the time. He was a bit of a smart-ass type, and somewhat mischievous. He was an easygoing guy who had a way with everyone. There's not a mean bone in his body. He was also a very good player on the field.

We had a lot of colorful characters on the Vikings during the time when I played. Keith Millard was another real character. He is a very dear friend of mine. He was a great player for us and was in the coaching business for a long time, and currently lives in California with his family. He was one of the more colorful characters we had on our team and somewhat volatile—but in a good way rather than a bad way.

Floyd Peters was our defensive coordinator when Keith was there, and he knew how to push Keith's buttons—and Keith knew how to push Floyd's. And they did it from time to time. There were a lot of conversations and banter that went on between them. They just knew how to get under each other's skin.

I remember one Saturday morning when we had a light workout before a game. We were sitting in the meeting room and Floyd was kind of picking at Keith. Pretty soon Keith started back at Floyd, and it kept going until Keith got up and walked out of the room. He stormed out of the meeting room and was gone. He got into his car and drove it up over a 20-foot bank, and later showed up at the hotel like nothing had happened. He could flip a switch and become upset.

But I will say this about Keith: he could flip a switch in a game and become unstoppable. He was a great player and had some dominating years with us.

I had some great mentors with the Vikings during my playing days. Wally Hilgenberg was a good voice of reason. He had been in the league a long time and became a good friend. Jeff Siemon was the starting middle linebacker when I arrived, and although we didn't spend a lot of time together outside of football, I had a tremendous amount of respect for both of them and how they prepared and carried themselves. Matt Blair was an outstanding leader, excellent player, and someone I admired. Even though I was the new kid on the block they were always there for me to answer questions or help any way that they could. They were always very professional in their approach.

Jim Marshall was a phenomenal leader and player. He never missed a game. He was always there on Sundays, and he had that aura about him—and the wisdom that came with all his experience. Bud entrusted Jim with the football team, to make sure that everyone was on the straight and narrow and focused on the task at hand.

There were a lot of veteran players on our football team for me to emulate. I got to see how they carried themselves on and off the field. It was a great time to come into a veteran team, to see how they worked and prepared and determine what I needed to do to get myself prepared to play every Sunday.

CHAPTER THIRTEEN

Rivals and Teammates

When I think of the best of the best among the players that I played against, I would have to start out with Jim Langer. He was the best center that I ever faced. Jim played for the Dolphins for many years and then finished his career with the Vikings. He was a great player for a long time. He was super smart and a very down-to-earth guy. He was extremely strong and had a very high football IQ. Jim was very quick and durable. All the years he played he was a steady, methodical guy. Jim was from Royalton, Minnesota. He was just a good old country boy, very unassuming and a real nice person. He was a big-boned guy with thick ankles and thick wrists and great forearms. He was a well-built individual for the position and he did an outstanding job. And of course being in the Pro Football Hall of Fame speaks for itself. He passed away in 2019.

With regard to other linemen, I practiced against Ed White for many years before he went to San Diego. Ed was a great guard who was as strong as a bull. Ed had the typical guard makeup: strong, fast, agile, and as overpowering as it gets.

There was also of course, Randall McDaniel, who may have been the best guard ever to play the game. He was a phenomenal player. He had this cockeyed stance but could run like a deer and was as strong as an ox. Randall was 295 pounds, small for today's game, but what a tremendous athlete he was. He had great hands, great feet, and a great temperament. He absolutely toyed with me when I was at the tail end of my career. The battles that he and Johnny Randle had were unbelievable. To watch the two of them go at each other in various drills was something to see. I truly think Randall was one of the greatest, if not the greatest, offensive lineman ever to play professional football.

Jimbo Covert of the Bears is another of the best I ever played against, as was Jackie Slater. They were both Pro Bowl and All-Pro players who were outstanding at their positions. These guys were players that gave all they had game in and game out, and were the best at what they did. I didn't get to see these guys as often because they were always blocking on the perimeter—which was probably a good thing for me. I matched up more with the guards and centers, so I didn't have to face them.

At tight end, the best I ever saw was probably Russ Francis of New England. He was a great football player and could basically do everything that a tight end was supposed to do—and he did it in outstanding fashion. Another was Steve Jordan, who I mentioned previously. Steve was very smart and savvy, could run, and had a very productive career.

Charlie Sanders of the Detroit Lions was another exceptional tight end. He later became a scout for the Lions. He was a great guy with a big personality, very competitive on the field, and could really catch and run with the football. I know that he and Wally Hilgenberg really had it in for each other and battled for years. They had their moments, that's for sure. My guess is they didn't like each other, and there was a bone of contention between Wally and Charlie every time we played Detroit.

One of the best players we faced was Wally's nephew, Jay Hilgenberg, who was a center for the Bears. Jay was one of those guys who was durable and dependable—a player that Bud would have loved. Jay was as steady as they come; he was smart and ran the show up front. He was a little bit undersized, but had good balance and great quickness. He was very competitive. You knew when you played him that he was going to give you his best shot.

There were so many great running backs who came through the league while I was playing. Walter Payton goes without saying. As do Eric Dickerson and Barry Sanders. People ran the football a lot back then, and with those kinds of players in your team's backfield, why wouldn't you run the ball? I'd also add Franco Harris, Larry Csonka, and Earl Campbell. We didn't play their teams that often—a fact for which I am grateful—but they were all incredible backs. William Andrews down in Atlanta was another outstanding running back. I know I'm leaving players out but there were probably 15 to 20 backs who were very tough to play against. We had great backs on our own team as well, particularly Chuck Foreman.

At the wide receiver position, there was Jerry Rice and Dwight Clark of the San Francisco 49ers and Lynn Swann and John Stallworth, both tremendous receivers for Pittsburgh. Those guys come to mind immediately and were all terrific. James Lofton had great ball skills and always seemed to produce against us; he was definitely underrated. Harold Carmichael of the Philadelphia Eagles was a great player for many seasons. He was a big target and a huge matchup player.

At quarterback, Terry Bradshaw of Pittsburgh was one of the best. He won a lot of Super Bowls for the Steelers under coach Chuck Noll. Joe Montana probably stood out the most. He had a great career with the 49ers and benefited from the right scheme and system to fit his talent. He wasn't the big-armed guy, the big mobility guy, or a scrambler, but he was so smart and savvy. He had impeccable timing getting the ball to his receivers and knew how to throw to them as they got open. He was a really heads-up quarterback. His talent was immense and he had complete command of the offense. He was, simply, a game changer. He was a true franchise quarterback, and those guys are hard to come by.

Dan Marino of the Miami Dolphins is another who fits into that category. He wasn't quite as mobile as Montana but he had a big arm and could really throw the football. Jim Kelly, a great player for the Buffalo Bills, was tough as nails and had the kind of grit that makes a good player a great one.

Fran Tarkenton, who played for us, was another of the best. He had tremendous scrambling ability and was very intelligent. He found ways to get the ball to people and had great vision and creativity in his approach. Tommy Kramer was one of the most competitive players that I have ever known. He had a tremendous arm, with great touch in both the deep game and the short game. He had some injury trouble late in his career, but he had a great feel for the position and was a natural.

On the defensive side of the ball, a few come to mind as being the best of the best. Charles Haley is one; he played in Dallas and then San Francisco. Howie Long of the Raiders was another great player. And Reggie White of the Eagles and Packers was one of the best ever. He was just a phenomenal player who earned every single accolade that he ever received.

The Bears of the 1980s had Richard Dent, Steve McMichael, Dan Hampton, and Mike Singletary. The Refrigerator, William Perry, was another great player who could dominate the inside rushing game even though he wasn't much of a pass rusher. That team they had when they won the Super Bowl would have been a really fun team to have played for. I always felt I would have enjoyed playing for Mike Ditka. I think those Bears teams really enjoyed the game; football was a blast for those guys. They had great chemistry.

The defensemen that get most of the accolades are the guys who rush the passer. So when I came into the league, guys like Jim Marshall, Alan Page, Keith Millard, and Carl Eller were all highly regarded—and they were right there for me to watch and enjoy as a player. It's neat to be able to say I was on the team and played with these greats of the game.

Ronnie Lott of the 49ers was certainly an intimidating player. He was a very physical guy with great range and striking ability who played with tremendous intensity. He was just fearless. I played in the Pro Bowl with him and he was the same guy during that game that he was during the season—very intense, all business, and just so physical.

You could certainly throw Joey Browner into the mix of great players too. He was an outstanding player for us for a number of years. He had all of the physical abilities that you need to play the game. He could run, was a great athlete, and could play in the box or in space. He really could do it all.

Jack Tatum of the Raiders was a hit man for sure. In today's game he probably would have been tossed out of a few games and garnered some hefty fines—he was a very physical player. He had great contact balance and was a striker. I'm sure receivers did not enjoy coming inside knowing that Jack Tatum would be there waiting for them. I mean, he could really lay the wood to you. He was a terrific player for a long time.

There are just so many great players I encountered in the league over the years. It is hard to get into names without missing some. When I think of rookies who have come into the league, the first one I think of is Randy Moss. He is kind of *the* marquee guy. When Randy came into the National Football League, he tipped it on its ear. He was sensational. As a young player, he changed the game, which is incredibly difficult. He became a threat like no one in the league had seen before.

This young kid, Justin Jefferson, has started off strong for the Vikings. It looks like he could have it all. He is crafty, fast, fluid, and a great route runner. He knows how to play the game—and that's just the way Randy was when he came into the league. Randy was bigger and faster than Justin Jefferson. You could not overthrow him. I mean he was six foot four inches with long arms and always had another gear.

Believe it or not, four teams passed on Justin before he was selected in the draft at No. 22. I will say that the receiver position is a very hard position to evaluate, but Jefferson was unquestionably pro-ready when they drafted him. He has been an outstanding player to this point and has a big upside. Stefon Diggs was a great player for us and is doing very well in Buffalo, but this kid Jefferson is a great find. He may not be as quick as Stefon but he has a very bright future.

Now I want to talk about one of my great friends, Keith Nord. This section of the book is very important to me because Keith was

Getting ready to blow the Gjallarhorn. (Courtesy of the Minnesota Vikings)

Being inducted into the Vikings Ring of Honor is an extraordinary honor and privilege. (Courtesy of the Minnesota Vikings)

In my second career, as a scout with the Vikings.

Watching from the sideline with Vikings owner Zygi Wilf. (Courtesy of the Minnesota Vikings)

Meeting the press with head coach Mike Tice at a draft event. (Courtesy of the Minnesota Vikings)

As far as I'm concerned, this group is the best scouting team in the NFL.

My wife, Jenny, is the love of my life.

Then and now: our kids, Jack, Sam, and Jessie.

Our lake house is our
happy place.

I'm a happy grandfather these days. That's me and J.J. above, and riding the lawnmower with Janie, below.

My wonderful family.

a good friend and great teammate. When he came to the Vikings he found a way to get his foot in the door, and you couldn't kick him out. He was always in the facility. He was tough. He was a fighter. He was very intelligent. He was 100 percent all of the time, and was with us for seven years. Keith was in a fight almost every day during training camp and it didn't matter if it was Chuck Foreman or a camp receiver. His intensity was through the roof and he left it all on the field, always.

Keith was about 195 pounds and about six feet tall, not huge by NFL standards, but he could run and was a very good athlete. He was probably a better athlete than a lot of people gave him credit for. He returned kickoffs and was the backup punt returner. He was tough as nails and had a good career. He got beat up toward the tail end of it, but he was certainly an achiever. He played above his abilities and found a niche that was unfortunately cut short by injuries and some bad breaks.

He played college ball at St. Cloud State and came to the Vikings as a free agent. Whenever I went into the weight room, he was there. Every day for him was a challenge and nobody was going to outwork him. His attitude was off the charts. I think we had some of the same traits and the same mindset. I was a ninth-round draft pick who worked my way onto the roster pretty much the same way he did. I suppose that's why we connected. We became very close friends. For one thing, we crossed paths often. He was a gym rat; I was a gym rat. We were always hanging around the facility trying to improve our game. I know he had a chip on his shoulder, and it served him well.

Keith was one of Bud's favorite players, not least because he went 100 miles an hour all the time. When he walked through those doors, you knew what you were going to get. That was Keith. That's the way he lived his life and conducted himself, and Bud was a stickler for reliability, dependability, and durability. When I heard he was sick I tried to reach out to him but failed to connect with him before he passed away. I regret not having more time with him. I miss you, my friend, and always will.

I don't think there was ever a team that I didn't want to play against. There were always players on certain teams that caused concern, but no team that I hated to play. There was a handful of players who played by their rules and would go against the call of duty, but not to the extent that I ever felt they wanted to end an opponent's career. I honestly don't think any player would deliberately try to hurt someone so they could not play again. Cheap shots would happen from time to time, but most of our rivals were tough, hard-nosed players who had a certain amount of respect for each other and the game.

Mike Ditka was the Chicago Bears coach for many years. Buddy Ryan, who was our defensive line coach in my first year, ran the Bears defense under Ditka. The Bears were a physical group that loved to run the football, and they had one of the very best who ever played the game in Walter Payton. He was a tough guy to face twice a year. He was extremely competitive and certainly a challenge to contain. He had some big days against us. When you competed against him for three hours it was a tough job, but when it was over, the respect and admiration was always there. He was an amazing football player.

I enjoyed the challenge from Walter and I knew he was going to get his due. Likewise, a back like Barry Sanders from Detroit could do amazing things with the ball in his hands and could embarrass you with ease. I think our division rivalries were extremely competitive, but always tinged with mutual respect.

When we played the Bears, they had great players on both sides of the ball. Payton, of course, along with Mike Singletary and Dan Hampton for the defense—both excellent football players. Dick Butkus was a phenomenal player with them for many years. He was big, very physical, and he played the game angry. Some of the highlights you can see of him are incredible. He could have played today. He was so physical and so ornery and mean and nasty—just a great football player. He could just thrash people. And he could really move for a big guy. I know his career got cut short with knee injuries, but what a special player he was. Mick Tingelhoff once said, "It was a beautiful sunny day and I came up to the ball and it was soaking wet. Butkus was spitting all over the ball." The Bears had so many exceptional players that it is hard to name them all. I had a lot of respect for them as to how hard and how well they played.

I played against Larry McCarrin, the center for Green Bay, for many years. He also played at Illinois when I was there. There was always a friendship, but our rivalry stood tall. He was one of those guys—when you played against him you knew you were going to be in a fight all day long. At the end of the day, you could feel good about your day's work with no hard feelings, as long as your team was on the winning end.

I always had a great deal of respect for Chris Spielman, the former Lions linebacker. He was a warrior. He played so hard—he gave 110 percent all day, every day. Chris was really a very special player. I think we had a similar style of play in that we played to the whistle on every snap, game after game. I would like to think that I was perceived that way—and I certainly know that he was. I can remember a game we played in Detroit: we won the game, but he was all over the field making tackles. I bet he had 20 or more tackles before the game ended. He never gave up on a play, and was the heart and soul of their defense. Afterward I walked up to him and told him how I admired his effort and how he played the game. I had a tremendous amount of respect for him.

Earl Campbell was an absolute beast of a running back. His thighs were as big around as your waist and he was so powerful and strong. He was another back who could embarrass you, like Payton and Sanders. I never wanted to get embarrassed, but he could do that to you. He could run around you or through you. He was the most physical player that I ever played against. Fortunately, we didn't have to play against him very often. Earl was one of those guys: you knew you were going to be on the losing end on some of the hits. What a physical player he was.

Another guy that we didn't have to play against very often was Eric Dickerson. He was big, fast, physical, and strong, and he could outrun you, run over you, and make you pay the price. Tony Dorsett of the Dallas Cowboys was another great back. He could beat you with his speed and quickness more so than his power. I recall he had a 99-yard run against the Vikings.

I always felt no matter what time in the season we were playing or what our record was, my job was to give all that I had every game, and I had to take pride in my performance week to week. It never made a difference to me what the score was or where we were in the standings. I felt I gave my very best. It was my job to be consistent. You can never get that time back or run that play over again, so you have to just go out and do the very best that you can each game. You just have to play until the game is over and then see how it shakes out.

There were some teams that we had trouble matching up against, and one of those teams was the San Francisco 49ers. During their heyday and Super Bowl dynasty—except for one game in 1987—we seemed to always have trouble with the 49ers. They had so many great players: Joe Montana, Jerry Rice, Dwight Clark, and Roger Craig, just to name a few. They were also a very well-coached football team on both sides of the ball. We struggled with the Dallas Cowboys for a lot of the same reasons.

Every win felt great, but the biggest win might have been the win against the 49ers in the 1987 playoffs. No one gave us a chance to win the game, and we did. Anthony Carter had a huge day, and Wade Wilson played exceptionally well too. Isaac Holt and Carl Lee covered their receivers all day. We were heavy underdogs in that game and came out of it with a great win.

The biggest disappointment of my playing career was the championship game that came just a week later. If we had won the game, we would have been in the Super Bowl. We had a great playoff run. We went on the road to New Orleans and beat them, then went out to San Francisco and beat them, and were ready for Washington. It was a game that could have gone either way. We had the opportunity to tie the game at the end, but unfortunately it didn't work out for us. That was probably the game that sticks out for me the most.

There were so many exceptional players who played in the same time period I did—players like Lawrence Taylor of the New York Giants, Harry Carson of the Giants, Ted Hendricks of the Oakland Raiders. There were guys who you admired and you followed their playing careers because you knew how good they were. We had a mutual respect for each other. When you are playing against guys of that caliber, you watch them on and off the field and just know how special they are.

One of those teams that was special in its own right way back then was the Oakland Raiders. They had some unique characters, cast-offs from other teams who joined together in Oakland to become an intimidating group. Guys like Lyle Alzado and others formed one rugged, physical football team. They had some great offensive linemen including Art Schell. Ken Stabler was their quarterback, and they had a bunch of rogues on the team that kind of went against the grain. But they showed up on Sundays and knew how to win. Their head coach, John Madden, was certainly a character himself. They always looked like a team with a lot of confidence and they found ways to win championships.

On the Vikings, I competed against some great offensive players in practice. As I've said, they were a very veteran football team back in 1977. Fran Tarkenton was the quarterback, Chuck Foreman was the highlighted running back, and Mick Tingelhoff, the Hall of Fame center, had been there forever as well. Ron Yary would become a Hall of Fame right tackle and Ed White was a big, physical player, one of the early 300-pounders in the league. Ed was full go every day of the week—even on Fridays, which was supposed to be kind of a gear-down day. Ahmad Rashad and Sammy White were there too. We were very talented but an older team.

So many of the guys I played with would be considered greats of the game. Randall McDaniel, Gary Zimmerman, and Tim Irwin were fix-tures on the line forever. Tommy Kramer became our quarterback after Fran retired and was a great player for us. Steve Jordan was another. You play against those guys every day at practice and it kind of makes game day a little easier. Those were some of the all-time greats, and guys I feel proud to call friends and lucky to call teammates.

We had so many great leaders when I came to the Vikings, and as my career wore on I had to do my part to help the younger players on the team. Walker Lee Ashley, Chris Martin, and David Howard were all younger players, along with Ray Berry and Mark Dusbabek. They were there to win a job and make a living. You did what you could do to help them, but also remembered that you needed to keep your own job. We were a close-knit group and there didn't seem to be any rivalries among us. We had good communication, and I would consider all of them very good friends to this day.

Even at the end, I don't believe there was any positional rivalry. Ray Berry was obviously going to take my job, and I knew that. In my last season, as I said, I would start the game and then Ray would come in and play most of it. Although that was a tough pill to swallow, I certainly understood it. I didn't begrudge him for taking over that spot in the lineup. It's a team sport, and you do what you can to help the team win; if that was the best scenario to help us win, then so be it.

I never really considered myself a mentor off the field but I was there if a young player needed anything, and I think they knew that. I always felt that if someone needed something from me, they would ask. I was available. But on the Vikings, everyone kind of took care of their own business for the most part and didn't seek a lot of help from veteran players.

I made All-Pro three times and was selected for the Pro Bowl twice. It was never expected and always an honor to be chosen, but as long as my teammates and the Vikings were pleased with my play and performance, the rest was just a bonus.

I think the All-Pro teams were voted on by the media and the Pro Bowl team was voted on by the players and the coaches. I recall filling out ballots. But unless you study the opponents to great lengths, the whole thing kind of becomes perfunctory. I wasn't really aware of exactly what type of season everyone was having, so it was kind of a write-in vote for the guys who made it the previous year. I'm not by any means bitter about it and I never felt slighted. Those honors were great experiences that came late in my career.

I really enjoyed going to the Pro Bowl. We got to go to Hawaii to play football. The schedules were minimal and the actual in-practice time was minimal. You weren't butting heads before the game or practice. I was honored to be a member of the team. I got to know the guys more so than I could have on game day. It was overall a tremendous experience. I was very proud to be selected. I never expected to go, so when my name came up, I was thrilled to say the least.

Injuries in the National Football League can be catastrophic. It can mean an early end to a career or long periods of time off the field. I had my share of broken fingers, shoulder problems, and stingers in my neck when my shoulder and arm would go numb. After contact I tried to play through it, but at times I had to come out of the game for a play or two. Injuries are a part of the game and all relative, and we didn't play through any more injuries than players do today. Players are taken very good care of by the team doctors and the trainers. When I was playing I think in some cases guys tried to tough it out more than in today's game, but the teams and the league take excellent care of their players. They try to protect the players the best they can, and they always have. Everyone is very cautious. Obviously there are more safeguards today than in the past, and that's a good thing.

Officials have not changed a lot. I understand that they have a tough job. They have to make split-second decisions and there is always that thing called human error. And then there's the matter of perception: if the call is against you, it is wrong, and if the call is in your favor, then they have done a great job. It is definitely a no-win job.

Some crews were easier to work with than others. Some were more flag-happy than others, but for the most part I thought they all did a decent job in a tough sport. They get graded on performance just like we do.

Players can bitch and moan as much as they want but not to the point where it throws someone off his game. There would be times that you would disagree with a call, but back then arguing rarely ever worked. Typically you would lose that fight. Today it is quite different with all of the instant replays and going under the hood. Calls are over-turned, and I think that's good for the game. It gives more than one or two people a chance to look at the call and see if it needs to be changed. More people get involved in the process; that's been good for the game.

Other changes to the game have had a good impact. The two-point conversion has been good for the game. The Vikings have certainly used it to their advantage under Mike Zimmer a few times over the years. That's kind of a gut call, and a tough one. The coaches have only 40 seconds to decide to go for the two points, unless they call a timeout. A lot of times they do it to win a football game or to stay within a certain margin, but it is often a very difficult call. There can be a lot of risk involved, and you can end up the hero or the goat. But I definitely think it has been good for the game.

The kicking game has changed too. For instance, the league has increased the yardage of the extra point. That may put more money into the pockets of the better kickers, but it has also changed the extra point from what was almost a gimme to putting a little more pressure on the kickers to make it. I think it has been good for the game that it's not automatic anymore. And when your team misses one of those kicks it can dramatically change the tempo of the game. The kickoffs are much more routine in that the kickers usually kick the ball into the end zone for a touchback. Still, even though the league is trying to avoid injuries on the kickoff they still have about two to three returns a game, which can be pretty exciting. Teams that have a great return man can certainly change the game and their field position.

Football is a very physical and violent game that is played by big, athletic people. I know that the rules and regulations that are set for the game are in place to try to protect the players, but the game will always have a risk to it. When you run full speed and collide with people, things happen. I think there is emphasis on trying to protect the vulnerable players who play in space, like the wide receivers and the runners. I'm all for flagging people for late hits and cheap shots, but it is hard to run full speed at someone and not hit with your helmet. I think it has been a good change to the game, but there is a fine line between intentional and unintentional. I know I would have had trouble adjusting to a rule like that. Our job was to get people down, and that's what I got paid to do. I know I would have adjusted, but it would have been tough.

I have been with the Vikings organization for a long time, and one of the best things the organization has done is its community Tuesdays. The work that players do out in the community is a wonderful thing, and a great experience for both the players and the community. I used to love the days when the organization built playgrounds for the kids.

Just to see how the kids reacted to it was so rewarding. It gave me time away from the job and an opportunity to give back. I give a lot of credit to these guys who do a lot for the community. It is not required, but so many of the players have embraced it. Helping people is a good thing. To just see the glow on a little person's face is reward in itself.

I was with the Minnesota Vikings for a total of 42 years and they are a very special organization to me. I have a lot of people who I call friends and care deeply for, and I have always felt that I was very well treated by the organization. To have played for the same organization for 14 seasons and then been with them in the scouting role for 28 years was a gift. I absolutely cherish this organization and everybody in it.

The Pro Football Hall of Fame is the highest honor any player could achieve playing in the National Football League. Those honorees are the best of the best, and if I ever did come up for consideration I would be extremely proud. That said, I think I was a good player for a great organization, but I have never considered myself a Hall of Fame candidate.

Until Jim Marshall is elected to the Hall of Fame, I feel there is a flaw in the process. I feel strongly that Jim should be in the Hall. A guy that played as long as he did without ever missing a game is extraordinary; it is remarkable and unheard-of. He is such a great guy, a true leader, and a great player. He could run like a deer for such a big guy too. I truly believe that they have done Jim a huge disservice by not inducting him into the Hall of Fame. I hope he gets the opportunity to get there, because he certainly deserves it.

CHAPTER FOURTEEN

The Coaches

I think a great football coach has to be a great leader. He has to control his staff and players and has to be a great communicator. He has to have exceptional knowledge of the game and has to be a good people person in order to manage the different styles and attitudes. But first and foremost, he has to be in charge. There can never be a doubt as to who is in charge.

There was never a doubt as to who was in charge when Bud and Burnsie were head coaches. They have to be able to protect as well as inspire the people surrounding them. Some guys are just born to be head coaches and some are not.

When I was in high school, my head coach was Don Watson. I mentioned earlier that Don was a short, sawed-off guy with a crew cut, loud voice, and a big personality. He was also a very good friend of our family. He was the guy who I looked up to early in my career. He was somewhat flamboyant, but he knew how to get people going. If he wanted to be tough, he could be tough. And if he wanted to laugh, he could do that too. He made the game fun, and as a young player I

really enjoyed playing for him. He brought both work ethic and relationship building to the game. When you are a young person at 14 or
15 years old, that makes an impression.

I got recruited by John Pont at Indiana and Bo Schembechler at
Michigan. Both of them were great coaches, but I didn't get to know
them well enough to be able to have a strong opinion about them.

Gary Golden was the defensive coordinator at Illinois and recruited
me. He was a very fiery individual and he would get so worked up on
game day that he would have everybody in a complete lather before
the game. He was just one of those guys who loved the game and was
all about competing. He exuded confidence and loved to work and
to play. He was just one of those guys who made an impression on
people.

Another guy who stood out for me was our defensive backs coach,
J.C. Caroline. J.C. was a great player in his own right and I think he
could outrun most of our secondary even then. Another coach who
I really liked and respected was Dave Adolph, and I had a very close
relationship with him. He was our linebackers coach. He went on to
coach in the league for quite some time. He had that drill sergeant
mentality—he was all about football, all the time. He earned the
respect of the team and was also a guy you could go and sit down and
talk with anytime. I kept in touch with him for years and years after
I left Illinois. It was always great to see him, and I had a tremendous
amount of respect for him.

On the professional level, Mike Ditka is the one that I really
admired above the others. Don Shula was in the league and was a great
coach too. I would have liked to have played for Shula, but would have
loved to have played for Mike Ditka. He was a big, tough guy who

played in the league himself for a long time. He had a wonderful career as a player and a phenomenal career as a head coach for the Bears. He won a Super Bowl with them in 1986. He had a kind of flamboyancy about him that I think I would have enjoyed being around. I got to know him a little bit off the field, and he was the same guy. It would have been awesome to have played for him.

When it came to the draft, I'm not exactly sure how much Bud and Burnsie were involved; I was a player when they were coaching. But I do know that Bud got along very well with Frank Gilliam and Jerry Reichow, and I know that he had a lot of confidence in them and their drafting abilities. I know Bud looked at the players, as did Jerry Burns, but I don't think they engineered much in the draft. They both trusted Frank and Jerry to do their jobs—and they did them very well. Bud did not have a lot of roster turnover at that time, so there were not a lot of new players added from the draft. It was similar with Burns. Steckel, on the other hand, was much more involved because that was his personality.

Denny Green, who was head coach for Minnesota from 1992 to 2001, was a good man. He had been in the college game forever and had a lot of experience. He was ready-made for the pro game. He was somewhat protective of certain people and he had a close circle that he kept pretty tight.

He was a very good communicator. A good coach and a good motivator, he was a hands-on coach. He was one of those guys who would want to know about anything and everything that had to do with the football program. I wouldn't call him a micromanager, but he was really on top of his business. He knew what every aspect of the operation was and was very much involved in the draft, as was his staff.

Denny was set in his ways and he didn't care who didn't like it. That was the way he did business.

Mike Tice was the next coach (2001–05) and had a huge personality. He was a loud and affable character for sure. I always felt he was a good football coach. And he's a great friend. Mike had a great sense of humor and was a player's coach. He was fairly young when he got the head coaching job. I played against Mike, so he hadn't been in the ranks too many years when he got the top job.

He was the line coach when he got the head coaching job. He was passionate about the Vikings and the success of our football team. He and his staff were very much involved in the draft and always had a good sense of what was going on in that area. I always felt that if he had more time, I think he would have won more. But the Vikings did win with Mike and I always felt he did a good job. I think the players respected him too. He got along with people and knew when to turn it on and turn it off. He was very serious at times, but he could be very funny at other times.

Unfortunately Mike was hamstrung in many respects by ownership at the time, and had to do a lot with very little. Red McCombs owned the Vikings back then and was pretty tight with the purse strings. I don't think he really got the chance to perform the way I think he could have. He was very much involved in every aspect of the organization—not to the extent that Denny Green was, but a good amount. I think his head coaching career got cut short because of outside influences. When Mike left he went back to being a line coach for several years and had a long tenure in the league.

Brad Childress became the next head football coach in 2006, after the Wilfs took over ownership. Brad and I were at Illinois at the same time, so I knew him pretty well and had followed his career. Brad had good success and was a very good offensive mind. He had been on Andy Reid's staff and was a good coach and communicator. Brad and his staff were very involved with the draft. They were also very good about letting you know what kind of players they needed at which positions. He was easy to work with in that regard.

He was and still is a good friend. I thought he did a good job, but unfortunately he fell short. He went on to coach in the league for many years after the Vikings job. The last time I saw him, at the Combine a couple years ago, he was doing some consulting work with the Chicago Bears.

Leslie Frazier came along next, in 2010. He had been the defensive coordinator for the Vikings and had a very different style than any other coach the Vikings had previously. He had a quiet personality and was a very unassuming type of person. He was a very intelligent football guy and had played the game himself. He was a very good communicator.

He was a good football coach and an even better person. He was so different from the other coaches in that he was so even-keeled. He very seldom raised his voice and was a strong believer that he didn't have to yell to get his point across. He was more of a teacher than he was a disciplinarian. I think he was one of those guys who was interested in letting his coaches coach, and he was more of a game manager. He was involved in the drafts, knew and evaluated the players, and had his own perspective on each player by position.

It is always hard when these guys leave because of the relationships you form with them. There are so many things that happen that are beyond their control, which makes the head coaching position a very tough job. Coaches are ultimately responsible for who is on their roster. You have to be a very tough person to do it. Leslie was a lot like Bud in some ways, but Bud won games, and that's the difference.

CHAPTER FIFTEEN

When the Cheering Stopped

I don't know if I was different than anyone else when the cheering stopped. It was something that I had been doing for some time and I was very passionate about the game, so it was not an easy decision. I was 36 years old, which is *old* for a football player. I wasn't sure what the next chapter would be. I knew I was going to have to do something. I wasn't interested in or able to retire.

I hadn't spent a whole lot of time thinking about it when I was playing. I didn't even know what my options were outside of football. I was just going with the flow, not making any earth-shattering decisions.

As I mentioned, I vividly remember what my wife, Jenny, said to me one day: "What the hell are you going to do for the rest of your life?" That statement kind of got me going and led me to a candid conversation with Roger Headrick. Those conversations with Roger in the fall of my final season got me thinking about staying in the game. And as it turned out, I ended up doing just that for another 28 years.

After 28 years in the scouting department, I knew it was the right time to retire—for good. There was a little bit of a burnout factor that led me into retirement, and it felt right. Looking back now, 14 years as a player and 28 years as a scout, that's 42 years in football, all with the same team. That's something that is not done very often. That's a long time with one organization.

But I had spent so much time on the road that I was wearing out. Jamaal Stephenson was a bright young man who was fit and ready to take over the director's position. I felt like it was time for me to move on and start a new chapter in my life. In hindsight, with COVID-19 and all that goes with it, it would have been really hard for me to do my job.

A friend of mine once told me that you live your life in thirds. One-third is your early years, your education and preparation years. Then you have another third that is your career; in my case that would be my playing days and scouting. The final third of your life is your retirement years. That is where I am today, adjusting to life away from the game.

Retirement is a work in progress. I have been retired about two years as of this writing. I miss the people but not the grind. I want to get involved with the people and the community. I have talked to the Minnesota Vikings about getting involved in some of their chari-table activities, and to former Viking Greg Coleman, who is involved in many charitable enterprises such as the Bridge of Reconciliation, YMCA of the North Mentoring/Sports Program, the Man Up Club Twin Cities mentoring program, the the Lights-on Program, and the Roho Collective. There are some things I want to do to give back and also to fill some space in my life. This would all be on a volunteer basis, obviously.

My exposure to today's game is very limited. I am a fan of the game, that's for sure, but on Saturdays I have a lot to do so I don't watch much college football. Obviously I watch Vikings games, but not too many other NFL games.

I also don't break the games down like I used to do, much less get emotionally involved. Being a fan is a lot different than being a player or a scout. I still feel lousy when the Vikings lose, but it is somewhat fleeting and a bit easier to digest.

A lot of time when I was working I would purposely go on the road and arrange my flights so I would miss our game. It was just so hard. Nobody wanted to be in the room with me. No one wanted to be around me. I was a mess during games because I wanted the Vikings to win so badly. I was just so wrapped up in every snap, even though there was absolutely nothing I could do about anything that happened on the field.

Because of COVID-19, there are limits to our daily activities, but we keep busy. My wife and I, our kids, and extended family have all spent a tremendous amount of time up at our lake place in Wisconsin, remodeling and taking care of business. We have spent about five days a week up there the past few months, and it is Jenny's happy place. You know what they say: happy wife, happy life! She loves it up at the lake. We have a huge family history up there and it has turned into quite a compound: four cabins and close to 20 acres.

I still work out some, but not as much as I used to. I liked to go to the gym, but I'm a little leery in going back to the gym until things settle down some. I bought an elliptical and work out there when we are at home. I have not lifted a free weight in about eight months; I know that I have to get back to that again. I don't feel good about not lifting weights. But I'm one of those people that likes to go to the gym and be in that kind of an atmosphere as opposed to working out at home.

After I quit playing I had an opportunity to do some broadcasting. I worked a few preseason games, but to be honest I wasn't very good at it and it wasn't something that I was interested in. I did it to see what it was all about, but ultimately it wasn't something that intrigued me or fit my style.

Over the years I had the opportunity to meet a lot of players and coaches from other teams. I enjoyed those encounters but never was one to be starry-eyed about who I knew and met. Rubbing elbows with a celebrity was not for me. I guess I was more of a lunch-pail type of football player and always wanted to keep it that way. This Minnesota bubble that I have lived in for the last 44 years is enough for me.

I do a lot of autographs for people who send me things in the mail. The amount of fan mail I get every day of the year is amazing. I bet I get five to six items a day—jerseys, hats, and small helmets, but mostly football cards. I think I must have the reputation for always signing and returning everything I get, because I get it from all over the United States, and even other countries. I'm happy to do it. I appreciate fans' interest and their recognition of what I did on the football field. I have always appreciated Vikings fans, so I try to answer everything I get. Honestly, the volume I get now is more frequent than it was when I was playing.

When I got nominated for the Ring of Honor with the Vikings, it was a big shock. I never expected it to happen; I just did not put myself in that kind of elite category. I was tremendously honored by the decision. Just to have your name mentioned with the great players of the past, the great coaches and people of the past, it's all very special to me. The Ring of Honor is a very special tribute and something that I am very proud to be a part of. There are not very many people in the Ring of Honor, so just to be among the Tarkentons and the Foremans and the Ellers and the Marshalls and the Pages and the Blairs and the Buds—I mean, it's a very special list of people. It's something that I am extremely proud of and I always will be. I feel very fortunate that I have had the opportunity to get there. It is really unique to be mentioned in the same breath as some of those greats of the past.

When I found out I would be in the Ring of Honor it was 2009. It was a huge surprise. I was getting ready to go on the road after training camp when Rick asked me to stay for the owners and personnel meeting that Friday. I recall being perturbed because I was ready to leave to scout players. We were all sitting around a table and Zygi started talking to me. It was almost like he was scolding me for something, which was confusing. I really didn't know what was going on. Finally I realized he was saying that I was the next member of the Ring of Honor. Jenny and our kids were all there and it was a great moment. During the game when it was celebrated, Zygi spoke, along with my dad and others. The day was so important to me. It makes me very proud and honored to have shared that moment with my family. But it took a long time for it to sink in.

A few years later I was named part of the 50 Greatest Vikings. It was another great honor to be among all of those Hall of Famers and great players. Again, it is not something that I ever counted on and to be nominated is truly an honor. It was never something that I expected or felt like I deserved. That makes it even a little bit better.

I don't really think ahead much in my life and I'm trying to get this retirement thing down and figure out what is next for me. The one really good thing about it, though, is the time that I can now spend with my family. I was on the road so much that I missed a lot of things with them and I can spend the time now to enjoy all of them and catch up. We have already spent more time up here at the lake than we have in the last 10 years. Being with my wife and kids and now grandkids has been very rewarding.

It's nice not to feel the pressure of winning or losing on Sunday. I still watch the Vikings and cheer for them. I still feel the pain when it doesn't go their way, but it doesn't ruin my day like it used to. I feel for the people in the building and the fans, but life goes on. You have to start some new chapters in your life. The job was a high-profile job, and I did it the only way I knew how. I think it was the right way to do it, but now it is time to focus on other things, and my family comes first. I need to give back to them for all the sacrifices they made for me.

There are other things I need to do and want to do. I'm not there yet. I'm good friends with Wayne Kostroski, who is heavily involved in the fight against hunger. Chad Greenway does a lot of great community work, so I should talk with him. I know that the longer I drag my heels, the harder it is to get started so I'll have to find something soon.

The reconnection with my family has been great. The commitment to my career has always been front and center, and the family has kind of taken a back seat to that. Of course I am thankful for the opportunity that I had with the Vikings, but I am very thankful for the opportunity to spend time with my family. I want to be sure that I am there for my kids, grandkids, and Jenny.

I do have hobbies. I like to fish and hunt, but it is hard with COVID-19. I used to go fishing down in Arkansas every year, but I didn't get to go this year. I just started pheasant hunting again and went to Kansas last winter. My son and son-in-law are avid deer hunters and spend a lot of time in the stands in Wisconsin. I don't really like venison, so I am hesitant to kill a deer when I'm not going to eat it. My son shot his first buck, an eight-pointer, on our property last year and it is hanging in our cabin right now. It's kind of cool and I know he is proud of it.

I play a little golf, maybe five or six times a year. I enjoy it but find that four to five hours out on a golf course is too much for me, especially if I have work to do. I didn't play golf at all in 2020. I can't hit the ball like I used to and it gets very frustrating, but I still enjoy the game.

At times I do get somewhat bored, but not too much. I can always find things to do. I'm one of those guys that has to stay busy. For me the days go by quickly. We'll be at the lake and I'll look at my watch and it will be 2:00 in the afternoon and we'll wonder where the time went.

I am very content at this point in my life. We are very comfortable. We get to watch our kids and our grandkids grow up. We are healthy, everybody in our immediate family is healthy, and we are in a good place right now. My parents are still alive too, and my brother and sisters are doing well. Life is good. Even with the challenge of today's world and the pandemic, it's nice to wake up every day.

CHAPTER SIXTEEN

COVID-19 and the Game

The effect that COVID-19 has had on football mirrors the larger effect that it has had on society. The game hasn't changed from the standpoint of blocking and tackling, passing, catching, kicking, or any of the other aspects. The work ethic and the demands on the players, coaches, football staff, and the ownership are the same. But all of the other parts of the game have changed dramatically. It is a different way of doing business, that's for sure, and a huge change.

With no fans in the stands, I'm sure most of the teams feel like they have lost home-field advantage. The Vikings certainly suffered some in 2020 due to the lack of fan support. Training camp, off-season conditioning, interaction with people have gone by the wayside for the most part during the pandemic.

I'm sure it was a huge adjustment for the players and the coaching staff. In a game where there is so much close physical contact, I am amazed that more players did not get sick.

In training camp, there were no preseason games. Personally I'm so glad that I did not have to go through that in evaluating players to see who should and should not make your football team. The only look that you get at a player this season is to evaluate them against your own team. There is a finite amount of contact through training camp. You want to be sure that you don't hurt any of your starters and your valuable backups, so there are probably a number of players that got shortchanged along the way.

There was no way for the pro personnel department to evaluate players on other teams through their preseason games. The only way to evaluate those guys was to look at what they had done in college or in previous years. It was tough for them, I'm sure.

My guess is that it was also extremely hard to cut down our roster, especially considering they had so many young players and lost so many veteran players. Think about it for a minute: The pro personnel staff had the opportunity in the past to evaluate a player through as many as four preseason games, as well as their collegiate career. They would know the players inside and out. By the time a player got cut from a team, you knew the player well because of all the information you were able to gather. In 2020, the pro personnel for the most part had to look at tape from college games. Everybody was behind the 8-ball. I'm not sure that anyone really knew what to expect from the season until it started. It's a great credit to players and the coaching staff that they didn't seem to miss a beat. Those guys are all competitive.

When you look at the Vikings roster, you could say that it was somewhat of a rebuilding year. The team started out slow, but some of the young guys started to come along. We will have to wait and see what happens. From my perspective, it didn't appear that the Vikings altered much as the season progressed. The bottom line is that every team is always trying to bring in the best players they possibly can, and the rosters are always composed of a lot of moving parts.

With COVID-19, many more people have been working from home and it still remains to be seen what will happen from here on out. On the football side of it, it may be that some people will be allowed that option to work from home. That said, I'm sure the coaches and football staff will always be on-site. As far as the other administrative staff, perhaps some will continue working from home.

There is also something to be said about sitting next to a coworker and having a conversation on the job. The human element has been lost. At some point the NFL will have to reach a happy medium as things start to get back on track.

The scouting area in particular has been affected significantly—especially the college scouting staff. The way they're accustomed to doing their jobs, and the hands-on approach that they have to take in their profession are significant. It cannot be done virtually. I think most of the scouts would tell you that their personal contact with the people is the key ingredient to their work. It's a grind and it gets hard at times, but I think the majority of the scouts would tell you they like being on the road and talking to people in person. They like seeing players live and in practice. They like getting the information they get out of the schools.

All of the games today are available, so the process of watching of tape doesn't change much. But lacking direct contact with people is a dramatic change. Personally, I'm glad that I am out of it. I know I would have had a very hard time doing my job. First and foremost, you get a much better evaluation of the players when you are around them personally, when you see them physically, when you talk to sources in the schools about the individual's character and their work ethic. The scouts still get the information, but it's not the same. I also know that I enjoyed going to the office; it would have been extremely hard for me to cultivate the discipline it requires to work at home. It all would have driven me nuts.

I'm happy in this third stage of my life. My family and I spend a lot of time together, which is great. We all live within a 10-mile radius of each other, so we see each other a lot. You worry about the kids and grandkids and worry about them getting sick, so this has been a tough time. You do your best and hope we will all get through it.

CHAPTER SEVENTEEN

The Front Office

When we originally moved into Winter Park, we did not have a proper practice facility. The old office was on France Avenue, which I believe has since been converted to a crematorium. It was a very small building that housed the entire coaching staff, personnel people, and the business and public relations people.

The move to Winter Park was exciting—and necessary. The football operations were downstairs and offices for the coaches and staff on the business side were upstairs. We also had two practice fields and a turf field under an indoor bubble for inclement weather. The whole complex was state of the art at the time.

The current facility, the TCO (Twin Cities Orthopedics) Performance Center out in Eagan, is truly unbelievable. It is a huge facility that is off the charts. It's a sight to see, a sight to tour, and a great place to work. The commute was a little farther for me, but certainly worth it. The Wilfs didn't penny-pinch when they built it; it accommodates everyone very comfortably. And with all the construction going on around it—the hotel, businesses, condos, and apartments—it has become quite the complex for the Minnesota Vikings.

The players, training room, weight room, and the equipment staff are all on the first floor. And there is another section at the complex that houses all of the incredible Vikings memories—past coaches, players, and memorabilia. It honors the Hall of Famers and Vikings Ring of Honor players and much, much more. The history of the Vikings from its inception is all there.

The number of people on the Vikings staff has increased dramatically. Before I left it seemed like almost every day I would see somebody new in the complex. You would cross these people's paths during the day when you were going to breakfast, lunch, or dinner at the facility or walking the halls. I mean, the number of people has just kept growing and growing. It is certainly big business. It is absolutely amazing the number of employees that have been added to the roster, so to speak. It is a growing business for sure, and you have to grow your workforce accordingly. There was no way that I could possibly know everyone working there even if I wanted to. As scouts we were kind of segregated geographically; we were on the second level while most of the business employees were up on the third floor.

Mike Lynn was the general manger for a long time with the Vikings. He stayed away from the players unless it was contract time but was heavily involved on the business side. The operation was so much smaller back then, maybe 50 employees compared to more than 200 today. During the season, no matter who was in charge, it was all about football.

After the Vikings Eight ownership group, Red McCombs came in and bought the team. Red was a real fan. He was from Texas and loved his Texas Longhorns, but he was a car salesman. He didn't know a lot about the pro football end of it and operated the club on bare bones. He had a big presence, though. He was big, loud, and he was very outgoing. His philosophy in running car dealerships—being tight with the buck—made him a lot of money but hurt the Vikings in the long run. It was a very hard transition for a lot of people who were not used to his type of management style and made their jobs much harder.

Once the Wilfs came in—Zygi, Mark, and Leonard—things really changed for the better. When they bought the team it was truly a blessing in disguise. Anytime you have ownership changes there is always concern from employees about what will happen next. There is always the potential for a complete overhaul to every department as well as huge personnel changes. In the beginning people were anxious, just like during any other ownership change.

The Wilfs have been fantastic. They are very successful people in the real estate business, as well as other endeavors. There was a grace period during the transition, but it just got better and better as time went by. We had to see how they were going to run the team, what their vision was, and basically how they were going to do business. Fortunately for the Vikings the Wilfs are fabulous owners. They are very supportive of their staff. They are very honest, open, and transparent people.

They have been really good for this organization and great for the community. They are all kind of an open book. If I wanted to pick up the phone and call Zygi, Mark, or Lenny I would feel very comfortable doing so, even now. They are all very approachable people and they are very hands-on. They are the type of owners who want to know what's going on. They are very interested in the day-to-day operations, and obviously interested in the football team. I remember their first Christmas party with the Vikings, their first year owning the team. I got a chance to talk with Zygi. I told him, "Try to stay out of the football business and let the people who know what they are doing run the show. And if you don't think they are doing a good job, then fire them and get someone else in here to do it—but don't do it yourself." I don't know whether he took it to heart or not, but it has pretty much been that way from the start.

They don't hold grudges and are fans as well, but they are first and foremost owners. Being kept abreast of the daily business is expected from people in the organization, and I know Rick and Mike Zimmer respect it. But everyone knows that if you make too many mistakes, you are going to have a hard time keeping your job. It is a very high-profile business that is out there in the public eye for everyone to see.

Every year you have to prove yourself. The Wilfs are very prideful people. They want to win championships. That being said, they are good for the organization, good for the fans, and I admire their openness and honesty.

I would hope they are in here for the long haul. They have been so good to work with and so good for the community, and we are extremely lucky to have them as owners of our football team.

I know that Rick Spielman has constant conversations with them about the team because they want to be updated on everything. They are good communicators, highly competitive, and very honest. Most of all they want to win, which is great for us. They are great for the team and the organization because they are extremely competitive people.

I have always liked the way they run the organization. They want to be informed of every decision made on the football side of things. And they will hold your feet to the fire because they want to know, should know, and deserve to know. Usually they buy into the football people's decisions. I think if I were in their shoes as an owner, I would try to be the same way. I would want to know what is going on too.

Besides the owners, Rick Spielman, our general manager, has a huge job to do. Rick is very accountable and very approachable. He has a tough job. I know how hard he works and that he puts his heart and soul into doing his job. He is the one in charge of the football aspects but keeps his hands in the business side of it as well. He works from dawn to dusk. He is always on the clock and never leaves any stone unturned.

Rob Brzezinski is in charge of the football operations and manages the salary cap. Rob has a great personality, knowledge of the game and system, and negotiates all the contracts. He is a very intelligent guy and is the voice of the financial side of the football business. He does a great job with the cap. He spends a lot of time at the facility and is in on a lot of football conversations due to their financial implications on the cap.

Rob is not an evaluator and doesn't want to be. He is extremely valuable to the organization and is a very honest, trustworthy, reliable person. He has history with Rick, having been with him in Miami. They worked together for quite a while and you can see the trust and passion they both have for their jobs.

I am very proud of the guys I worked with directly, and I give kudos to Conrad Cardano, with whom I cut my teeth in the scouting business. I love the scouting staff that we have assembled, and I was able to hire about half of the group that's currently there. They have been intact for a long time. You always feel good about bringing in quality people you can trust, and you know they will do their work day in and day out.

I am very proud of Jamaal Stephenson, the scouting director and my successor. He has a bright future in this business. He is a very hardworking individual and does an exceptional job. When I stepped down I was very happy that Jamaal got my old job. He was ready for it and he does a great job.

I am extremely proud that we were able to put together such a quality, diverse group of people to represent the club. They have all been such great fits. Some came from other teams, some came as interns from other organizations, but they all had some scouting in their background and they have blended together to make a great group within the Vikings organization. Everyone in the whole group is attached at the hip. They do an exceptional job and I am very proud to call them all friends.

When people like Brad Madson leave an organization after some 25 years, you really feel it. Brad was in charge of all of the community work that the organization does. He was such a wonderful community organizer, and so much of his work goes on behind the scenes. He was so full of energy, always with a smile on his face, and such a tremendous contributor. He was open and honest and a personable guy. When he asked you to do something, you did it because you knew it was important to him. Everyone liked Brad.

Bob Hagan is our vice president of communications and a great friend. My wife absolutely loves him to death. He is a very honest and loyal person. He has the right kind of demeanor for that job, as does his right-hand man, Tom West. They're both super guys. Bob has certain expectations when he walks into your office; you know he needs something. He is a good people person. He gets along with everybody and is never pushy. He does his job and he does it well, and above all you can trust what he does with any information you share. He has a very tough job and does it with great pride. I had my moments with the press during my playing days, so I know how hard they can be to deal with. Bob and Tom both do super jobs.

I was very blessed to be around such wonderful people. Everyone is there for the love of the game and the organization. They are well compensated and they earn every penny of it. Their hard work and dedication are worthy of the very highest esteem. You have to have big personalities to survive in this business, and they are very grounded people who are open, approachable, honest, and have unquestionable integrity.

CHAPTER EIGHTEEN

Loves and Passions

I mentioned my parents earlier, but I think it is time to say a little more about them. There is no question that the two biggest heroes of my life are my mom and dad. They were always there for us kids and shared and sacrificed so much. They were our biggest fans and are very loving and caring parents.

My one sister was a swimmer and the other ran track, and my brother played football and basketball. I played football and baseball. My parents were always there for each of us. You'd look up from whatever you were doing and there they would be. They were always on the go with four kids, but they always did it with so much love and passion.

My parents are the two people in my life that I always looked up to as heroes and role models. I also tried to model a lot of my behavior after my older brother, and although we didn't become tight while we were growing up, we are today. After he left the house and went off to college, our friendship and love for each other kind of blossomed. I feel the same way about my sisters. We have a close-knit family.

Outside of my family, through my high school years, I want to again mention our high school football coach, Don Watson. Don was very close to our entire family. He was funny. He was engaging. He was stern and he was strict as a coach, but he was very outgoing and just a great guy. He spent time with my folks outside of the game. My brother and I both played for him. He also attended some of my games at the University of Illinois and some of my brother's games at Evansville. He was a coach, a teacher, an educator—someone you looked up to and admired.

We had limited exposure to the pro game but did follow our local team, the University of Evansville. They had some really good basketball teams back then—and still do to this day. Jerry Sloan, the great former Utah Jazz coach, played at Evansville. I used to sell popcorn and cotton candy at the basketball games, so I was around their games and program growing up.

I had a couple of pro teams that I rooted for as a kid: the St. Louis Cardinals and the Chicago Bears. Dick Butkus held the middle linebacker post for the Bears for many years. Butkus was something else. When we kids weren't outside running around and playing, we would watch Bears games on television. You just had to admire the way Butkus and Gale Sayers played. Ditka was another big name that I always looked up to.

As a former linebacker, I really looked up to Dick Butkus. He may not have been the most athletic linebacker in professional football, but he was for sure the most ferocious. There were probably some players who were his rivals and maybe there were better athletes, but this guy was big, competitive, and such a physical presence on the field. He was in a category of his own. He could really move for a guy his size. He was about six foot three and around 250 pounds, and he played like his life depended on it. He was literally trying to kill people—at least it looked that way.

I got to know Dick through the years when I was playing at Illinois and then on the Vikings. Even after he was done playing, he was still such a huge presence, a larger-than-life type of character. I probably didn't emulate him as a player, but I sure did look up to him for what he had done on the football field. I'm glad I got to know him. He has that little edge to him, but he is also personable and outgoing. He is a good communicator and one of those no-nonsense guys who could see right through you if you were trying to feed him a line. He was an absolute pleasure to be around.

One of my interests for a short time was arm wrestling. For many years before I got involved, the NFL held an annual arm wrestling tournament, and the big guys had the upper hand. I represented the Vikings, along with Jim Hough. The first year that I went they had a lightweight division and a heavyweight division. This would have been around the early 1980s. Jim talked me into it.

I had never really done it before and was not a big proponent of arm wrestling by any stretch of the imagination. Then that very first year that I went with Jim, he hurt his arm. I went through the light-weight division, which I won! And then I had to go and jump up into his heavyweight division, and I won that too. I beat Ed White, who was with the Chargers then, and then I beat Joe Klecko of the New York Jets twice to win it. All I can say is fear is the great motivator. It certainly helped me out.

The next year, Jim hurt his arm again and I had to jump up in weight class again. This time, I had four or five contests in about an hour, and by the end my arm was shot. I ended up losing. If memory serves, I got second place and I believe it was Joe Klecko who beat me. It was always fun to see guys off the field. They are just regular people trying to make a living at the end of the day. I made some good friendships. Arm wrestling was a fun thing to do but it was not something that I ever trained for or was inspired to do. I probably just got lucky the first time out.

I have to mention my weight lifting once more because it was and still is a big part of my life. We went from the garage and sand weights to barbells and dumbbells. In high school it really helped with my physical development. Since then it has always been a significant part of my life.

Weight lifting was not a huge priority in general circles, but it really helped me along the way. Once I got to college, the weight lifting increased and became structured. It was very beneficial for me, and I liked it. It was fun and I looked forward to it. The way I trained and managed my weight was always one of my strengths. I know that I got good genes from my parents, but the weight training was very important to me because I know for a fact that it extended my career. When you are in a business where strength, agility, leverage, and resilience all matter, it is important that you stay on top of your business.

I still enjoy working out. I used to run a lot, three to four miles a day, and conditioning has always been important to me, but unfortunately I can't run anymore. My ankles and knees have kind of done me in. They are beat up to the point where I can walk and work out on equipment but that's about it. I just can't do it physically anymore. I would like to go out for a run and work up a sweat, but I can't.

I try to work out every day, but because of COVID-19, I can't go to the gym and work out, and that has been pretty tough on me. I need to get back into a routine again. It's important to me and I eventually will. I'm active and I'm busy, but it's not quite the same. I try to keep physically active because it is good for the mind as well as the body.

A year or so ago we had a tornado go through our lake property, as well as some straight-line winds that knocked down more than a hundred trees, so that has taken a long time to clean up and is still ongoing. I love to cut the grass, split wood, build fires, and things like that. My pole barn is full of so many grown-up toys that sometimes I wonder where they all came from. It keeps me busy and I enjoy the work.

CHAPTER NINETEEN

Extra Points

There are some points to be made about several subjects, so I put them here in this chapter as extra points, so to speak.

There has been a statement that has often been repeated through the years that 75 percent of NFL players are broke within three years of retirement. I'm not sure where those statistics come from or whether those numbers are even close to being accurate. They may be 50 percent or 25 percent, if even. There are a number of factors to consider. First, I would like to know if there is a cutoff between former players who played 5 years ago or 10 years ago or even 20 years ago. I believe today players are a lot better educated than they were in decades past. They have tremendous resources inside and outside the facilities to help them handle their money and take care of business.

You can look at some players who have gone through millions of dollars and ask, "How could anyone spend that kind of money?" Well, they can and they do, but I think those players are the exception rather than the rule.

Of course, it is a shame when that does happen. A lot of times they get really bad advice and are taken advantage of. They listen to family members rather than the people who are hired to help them. When it does happen it is a travesty, especially when there are people who take advantage of these players. There are people who lie to them and do careless things with their money. It is very sad to hear about it, and see what happens to some of these young men. Some of it is the player's fault and some of it is not.

There are players who get a large amount of money through bonuses or their salary and some of them get very careless and live very attractive lifestyles.

A lot of these players come from low-income families and have never had any money or been around it. There is often a lot of pressure from their families, which can lead to poor decisions along the way. They start giving handouts to uncles and aunts, their brothers or sisters or parents. I mean, how many times have you heard about players buying houses for their parents? It is an honorable thing to do, very noble, but the money can run out very fast—especially if they only play three or four years in the league. It can all be gone quickly if a guy isn't careful. It probably mirrors society to a certain extent, and it's too bad because football is a very short-lived career. On the other hand, it can be an unbelievable stepping stone for the rest of your life if you take advantage of it.

The Vikings offer fabulous services to the players. Les Pico does an incredible job with the players, advising them and assisting them in just about anything that they need. He runs the player program that mentors players in every sphere of their life. Les deals with off-the-field issues, whether financial or legal or familial. Through the team, a whole gamut of life lessons are available to the players if they want them. It's hard for some of these young guys to handle this business. As a professional athlete, you encounter so many parts of life that you have never seen before.

Players will face a number of people who want something from them, and they have to question whether they have his best interests at heart. And many of them do, and go out of their way to help these young men with advice, counseling, and guidance. You always have to be circumspect, though.

There are so many issues that these guys have to confront on a daily basis and on an annual basis beyond just playing the game. So if the people that the players have hired to run their business dealings are not quality people, they can take advantage rather easily.

Vikings players are encouraged to be involved with team assistance, and some of it is mandatory. They have individual meetings with the players, along with collective meetings. Basically what they are trying to do is be there for them and to offer them advice and counsel to assist them in their lives. Financial people are brought in, drug awareness people are brought in, and many others who bring information about what players may face, such as family issues and lifestyle issues.

Les is always on call and ready to assist. He is a behind-the-scenes guy who played and coached football in college, and he has a great demeanor. He also has a law degree and is there to provide help to anyone who needs it. He is simply a super person who can be trusted and does a great job with our team and players.

Every team in the league has a guy like Les who does the same thing. Their job is to try to help players navigate life outside of football. When you see where some of these players have come from, the fact that they can make it to this level is remarkable. It is astonishing when you see their history that they have even *survived* up to this point in their lives, much less thrived. A lot of these guys need help; they need a mentor and someone to look after them. For some of them it is very hard to adjust to the life. Some of them get it and some don't. I commend the league for supporting them and I commend the Vikings for the way they do it, because it is a great program and resource.

Another area I wanted to mention is the fact that there are some teams in the league that struggle over long periods of time. They change coaches and general managers on a frequent basis and they still end up losing. For whatever reason, they just cannot get over the hump. It is an easier hole to dig out of in today's world of professional football than it may have been years ago. Today we have both the salary cap and free agency, so there are opportunities to move forward, but winning in this league is never easy.

Fortunately for the Minnesota Vikings, we have only had one really bad season—and that corrected itself quickly. For the most part, our history has shown that we have always been competitive, and that's because there are great people at the top of our organization. It's hard to understand how it happens, but look at Jacksonville in 2020. They were a kick away from beating us recently and had a dismal season altogether. They fired their general manager and head coach.

To my mind, you have to have stability in the front office and on the coaching side or it won't work. When you have that, the team is always going to have a chance. There are always good and bad years, everybody will have them. It happens to everyone to some extent, but the good teams can bounce back. For that you need the leadership from owners, your general manager, and your head coach—it is a trickle-down effect. When you have good people in those kinds of positions, typically you are going to be successful.

It can take a long time to change the attitude in a building. You have to change the culture. I would assume losing can become pervasive just like winning does. There is a culture in all of these organizations that goes from the top down. It has to be a positive place to work if you want a winning culture. You have got to find a way to make people want to come to work every day. You have to grind every day. You have to sacrifice every day. I would assume in some of these places that it must be kind of a helpless feeling because they have not been able to establish that kind of positive culture.

Every time a team hires a new head coach, maybe it has a shot at changing the culture and maybe it doesn't—and then it's the same thing over and over. If you look at the talent across the league and you took the jerseys off 20 players and moved them around, they would be the same players on different teams. What I'm saying here is that the players remain the same and there is not a whole lot of difference in the rosters; it's all in how they are managed. (The quarterbacks are probably the only ones who would be an exception to that.)

Once you are on the bottom, it is incredibly difficult to get back to the top. I was never in a position to experience how people in losing organizations felt. I'm sure it's awful, but I don't know. They probably feel desperate and full of self-doubt, and it must be very hard to come to work every day. Their staff likely works just as hard as a winning team's staff, but for some reason it doesn't work.

I have been asked this question a few times: "Should my son play football?" I have one son who did. He started in the third grade, but he didn't really know what he was doing. My wife was not a big proponent of him playing football. When he was in the eighth grade he came to me and said that he didn't want to play anymore. I told him that he wasn't playing for me, and that he should finish out the season and then quit playing if that's what he wanted to do. That's just what he did, and it was fine with me, Jenny, and him. Football was not his cup of tea. We never have forced him to do anything he didn't want to do. Looking back, what I probably should have done is put a golf club in his hand. He loves golf and is a really good golfer. He played baseball and basketball as well.

My advice to parents is to let a kid play, especially if he wants to play. But when a kid is playing and just the parents want him to play, then it's wrong. There may be an underlying issue there that needs to be addressed. Football is a great sport but it's not for everyone. There is a fine line as to whether you should promote it or not. I didn't start playing until I was in the eighth grade, and that worked for me. I'm not a doctor or a specialist, so I don't really know when a kid should start playing, but I'm not sure that they should start at an early age.

There are pluses and minuses. I think the sport has done just about everything it can possibly do to keep the game safe. When you get to the later years, when the players are huge and fast and they collide, someone can get hurt. That's just the nature of the game. They have made changes in the equipment—and it is about as good as it could be—but people still get hurt. The game is probably a lot cleaner than it used to be too, but even with that, there still will be guys who get hurt. Just look at all the injuries across the league in 2020—although a great amount of that can probably be attributed to the lack of training camp and preseason games.

I think parents need to be open-minded. There is a time and place for everyone to play sports, football included. If the kid wants to play, I would say let him play. And for those that do and are good players, I would encourage them to play until they can't play anymore. What I am talking about here is graduating from high school to college to the professional level. The time to walk away is when you can no longer match up to your competition or to your teammates. When that happens, it is time to try something else.

When you look at the whole injury issue in football, obviously some of it is genetic, some of it is luck, the way people are built, the way people take care of their bodies…there are so many factors. Football is a very physical game at every level. Some of the injuries are career-threatening or career-ending. The ones that worry you the most are head injuries, and the long-term ramifications of those types of injuries. Safety is a huge focus at every level of the game, and people are doing everything they possibly can to minimize risk, but they will never be able to eliminate it.

I know Bud always talked about the fact that some players are just more vulnerable to injury than others. That seems to be true of CTE, though it is hard to figure out why some players are more susceptible than others. We don't know why, but it's true. It is sad to see that some players have lost their lives because of it while others go on without any problems.

During my career I had a few concussions. I guess we called it getting "dinged"—you get up and see stars and are kind of out of it. But I have never had any long-term problems from those hits, at least to this point in my life. Maybe I'm being a little naive, but I just tried to ride it out and it worked for me. I was never knocked out or had to be carried off the field.

Some injuries are so unbelievable, though. Take Teddy Bridgewater's injury for us a few years ago. He got his foot caught in the ground at practice and was hurt so seriously that he almost lost his leg. Eric Sugarman, our trainer, did such a great job with him that the leg was saved and fortunately Teddy is playing again.

I have spent time over the years volunteering for various organizations, such as the Special Olympics. I have a nephew, Max, with Down syndrome. He has a special place in my heart, so I have been involved in some of those charities. When I played, the team did not have the community programs that there are today, but I tried to find programs where I could give back.

The Make-A-Wish program is another. I was on the board of directors for a while, and I loved doing that. The program involves granting wishes for kids who have very serious health problems. Kids with cancer or very debilitating diseases are granted their wishes. The program helps the kids' families and the kids themselves by granting wishes that perhaps the family could never afford, such as going to Disney World or as simple as attending a sporting event and meeting a favorite player, or going on a camping trip or a family vacation. I haven't done it for a long time, but it was a very rewarding program for me.

CHAPTER TWENTY

Family

I met my wife at the Rusty Scupper. It was kind of our hangout in the late 1970s and early 1980s. It was right there at I-494 and France Avenue. She was a cocktail waitress there—with a degree in art history from Macalester College in St. Paul. In the beginning we were just friends. Both of us were in other relationships before we started dating, and had a very cordial relationship that stayed at the Scupper.

She is a very outgoing person, very smart and very good-looking. She is a beautiful person inside and out, so it didn't take long to fall in love and realize I wanted to spend the rest of my life with her.

After we got married, she became a stay-at-home mom. Later, when the kids were grown, she started working with disabled young kids in the Eden Prairie school system. She worked for a number of years at Eden Lake School and retired about the same time that I did.

She is a football fan, but nothing like me. Her parents were season-ticket holders and had Vikings tickets for a number of years. Her dad was a doctor and her mom was an educator and an artist. She went to games when she was a little girl, but I don't know if she ever had a great interest in football.

Once we met and eventually got married, she became part of the football culture. Football was my life and a part of hers too. She was more worried about me getting hurt and taking care of the kids at the same time than really enjoying the games, so she never got too caught up in the culture. Then later, when I became a scout, it was extremely hard for me to sit down and watch us play. Each game was three hours of complete torture. I was so wrapped up in everything for the team that I could barely watch the games. When I did, I watched alone. The successes and failures of the football team had become too much for me, so it was very difficult for me to even sit down and watch a game, let alone watch it and enjoy it with Jenny. She is obviously a Vikings fan and wants them to do well, but we are somewhat detached in retirement.

Jenny has basically put up with me for the past 35-plus years and raised four kids (with me being the fourth!). And with me on the road for so much of that time, it wasn't easy. She was just about a single parent for nine months out of the year. Even when I was at home, my mind was at work, so I wasn't much help with anything. Jenny is a great wife and grandmother. The kids are all doing well and are very successful. I was very fortunate to meet her and marry her. Now I look forward to us growing old together.

Our children are all the best. Our oldest, Jessie, is 34 years old. She was working full-time and raising two kids, J.J. and Janie. She was in marketing with Dairy Queen for a number of years and is now a stay-at-home mom with her third child, Jackson. Her husband, Nick, played football at Mankato State; he was a tight end and backup punter there. He is a project manager in the construction industry and does well. They live right around the corner from us, so we see them often.

My second daughter, Sam, is 32 years old, and is a single mom with a daughter, Penny. Sam was a character growing up. She and her daughter, at the present time because of COVID-19, live with us. She has been running a learning pod for about five kids out of our basement and is doing well.

My son, Jack, is 25 years old. My old friend Conrad Cardano and I had a couple beers one night and he really talked me into the idea of another child—and what a blessing Jack has been for us. He is a great kid who works for an insurance agency. He has been a great son, fun to be around, and a really nice person. He lives with his girlfriend, Abby, who is a physical therapy assistant. He is a big hunter and loves to play golf.

My four grandkids are all wonderful kids. I also have eight nephews and one niece. The youngest, Max, who I mentioned earlier, is very special to me and our family. He is a wonderful young man whom I love dearly.

We often took family vacations together over the years. We went to the Bahamas a few times and to the Pro Bowls in Hawaii. The biggest thing for us, though, has been my wife's family lake place on Bone Lake in Wisconsin. It's about 90 miles from our home, which is just perfect. The lake place has been in the family for almost 100 years, and we all love to be there. Now that I am retired we spend a lot of time at the lake.

I am firmly convinced that it has kept our family intact. Our kids love to go there, as does Jenny. It's a great place for all of us to be together. Both of Jenny's sisters have places there too, so it is one great family get-together when we are all there at the same time. We have close to 20 acres and about 800 feet of lakeshore. We are at the lake all the time in the summer and have finally been able to spend time there in the fall and winter.

I think the best thing about my family is how the kids have turned out. We have always tried to steer them in the right direction and not be overbearing parents. We have not tried to be tremendously controlling and allowed them to follow their own paths. We were there for them when they did good things and there for them when they did some not-so-good things. We tried to keep them on the right path toward success. They are all in the Twin Cities, and we like having them around. They have been great kids. They all have college degrees and great heads on their shoulders.

I think the pandemic has had a silver lining to some extent because we have all been around each other so much. They are happy and healthy kids. I probably don't give them the credit that they deserve, but I am so proud of each of them.

CHAPTER TWENTY-ONE

Final Thoughts

I'm one of those guys who would have played the game for free. Based on the way the salaries are today, maybe I *did* play for free. Seriously, though, football was a labor of love, both as a player and as a scout. The game fit my personality and my work ethic, and I was so passionate about both phases of my professional life that I looked forward to going to work every day. I enjoyed it so much.

The best part of playing was the competition. The camaraderie I had with my teammates and staff and the friendships that I made along the way have been so special to me. Every time I see those guys everything just comes flooding back. The time we spent together, the blood, sweat, and tears that you shed over the course of a game, a week, a month, or a year comes back. I had the best two jobs in football, no question.

The scouting part was equally rewarding. Building the roster to try to stay competitive was a major part of the job, making sure that the players fit what you were trying to accomplish both on and off the field. Being proud of these guys that we picked, especially if they turned out to be really great players or good players, or even backups was a special feeling. There is a certain sense of accomplishment that comes with it. Of course, the guys you remember the most are the guys that you missed on rather than the ones that you hit on. It's a funny business that way, but that's a part of it. The people that you work with and the endless amount of time that you put into the work comes with a price, but in the end it was all worth every hour spent. To see it all pay off is an incredible feeling—like none other.

I was as fortunate as anyone could be to have spent 42 years in a business that I loved.

Coauthor's Note

There have been many great players in the history of the National Football League and many great front-office staff, personnel people, and scouts. But how many of those people have put both together in a career spanning more than four decades? Scott Studwell has done it. He spent 14 years as a middle linebacker and 28 years in the scouting department, all with the Minnesota Vikings.

During his playing career he was known as a ferocious hitter. He liked to hit people. He thrived on it and he did it so incredibly well. Scott was as hard-nosed a linebacker as they come. During his illustrious career in Minnesota, he made a staggering 1,981 tackles. This is not a misprint. He made 1,981 tackles in his career, 500 more than the closest Viking.

Among his Vikings records are 24 tackles in a single game against the Detroit Lions in 1985, and 230 tackles in a single season, in 1981. For the University of Illinois, he remains second only to Dick Butkus in tackles and was named one of the Greatest Fighting Illini Linebackers in 2008.

After his playing career, he became an administrator and eventually a scout for the Purple. Traveling the United States for 28 years, he averaged 200-plus days a year on the road scouting players. He went into every single nook and cranny to find players. If you played any kind of football during those years, Scott likely knew who you were. He would scout as many as a thousand or more players a year in preparation for the NFL Draft. He was a tireless worker and one of the best scouts in Vikings history.

Setting aside for a second Scott's tremendous history as a player and a scout, he is also a tremendous person. There is no question that Scott Studwell is one of the nicest people that anyone would ever want to meet. He is a great husband, father, and grandfather. His whole life since retirement has been about his family, making up for all the years he was on the road scouting. He has done it well, spending a lot of time at home and at the family's lake place in Wisconsin. His priorities are in order.

Working with Scott on his book has been one of my most rewarding experiences. It has truly been an honor.

—Jim Bruton, coauthor

Afterword

Being married to Scott for 37 years and counting has been an adventure. Years ago my beloved granny said, "Look, dear, if I were 50 years younger I'd give you a run for your money." He's not only devastatingly handsome on the outside but he's got good stuff inside too. He keeps me level, grounded, and balanced with few words—always words of kindness but also truth, even when it's hard to hear. That's entirely necessary when raising a family.

Our kids, Jessie, Sam, and Jack, own his heart, and he theirs. Loyal. Kind. Dependable. Generous. Traits absorbed within from the good beginnings of his nuclear family. The role of patriarch to my extended family plus his quiet authority help keep us strong and together.

His fun, generous nature has made life a blast. He is a workhorse, whether on the field or at the cabin. He is filled with boundless energy. He never stops! He's either in motion or asleep. His hugs are worth a million words/tears. He's a baby whisperer. He is kind, one of the good ones. My rock. The adventure continues.

—Jenny Studwell

I guess I would start with my dad is my hero. And I know it sounds cheesy, but he is. I remember my mom always said, "Dads are always the ones kids adore." But I think adoration would be selling him short.

When I was a little girl, my teachers would ask, "What do you want to be when you grow up?" My answer was always, "The first female football player" because I idolized everything he stood for. He was tough but gentle, hardworking, dedicated, cool, kind, smart, articulate, loyal, respected, and when he spoke, everyone—and I mean everyone—would shut up and listen. Not only was he a great dad to his own kids, but he was also a willing father to those who needed it, whether friends or family members. He was always there to give a comforting hug and let those who needed it know how much he loved them, as if they were his own.

He pours his love into his kids and now he gets the same with his grandkids. As a parent it is so fun to see the bond he has formed with each of them, volunteering to take them to school, tagging along to flag football games, taking them for long tractor rides at the cabin. When my youngest son, who is more than a year old now, sees him he absolutely squeals with happiness! The kids love him as much as I do.

Dad was not a pushy parent when it came to sports. He encouraged us to play whatever sports we chose, and only asked that when we played, we really tried. I can't tell you how many times I was asked, "Do you have a brother? It must have been really tough having him as a dad." And truthfully, no, he could have cared less about what came of our athletic abilities, as long as we gave it our best.

Those that can get past the "football player Scott Studwell" are able to see what I have experienced as his daughter. He is just a great man, father, father-in-law, son, friend, and brother.

— Jessie Nalezny

As a dad, I couldn't ask for anything more. He is supportive, thoughtful, calm, kind, and reassuring. He conveys all of this in a quiet manner—strong and silent has always been his style. However, when he does speak, everyone listens. He gives the kind of hugs that make you feel safe; sometimes they even bring on happy tears. As great as he is as a dad, he is even more wonderful as a grandfather. He frequently runs to Culver's for custard, he drives the kids to school, chuckles at their bad behavior, and throws them high into the air. He loves his grandchildren. As my daughter says, "He is the nicest grandpa there is!"

—Sam Studwell